Chord Piano Is Fun!

Version 3

Instructional Videos that go along with each lesson are available for purchase at **www.chordpianoisfun.com**

by T.K. Goforth

Instructional Videos that go along with each lesson are available for purchase at **www.chordpianoisfun.com**

WELCOME!

THANK YOU for choosing "*CHORD PIANO IS FUN!*"

Have you taken piano lessons for years but have never been able to play popular music?

Have you only taken a few months of piano lessons, but really want to be able to play something that you enjoy?

Have you always wanted to learn to play piano by **CHORD** but never knew where to start?

If you answered **YES** to any of the above questions, then **CHORD PIANO IS FUN** is for you!

Having played piano for years, I wanted to find the perfect method to teach piano by chord. After hundreds of dollars spent, I decided that none of the products I purchased met my needs. So, I created a VERY easy to follow method book, which provides the basics on how to play chord piano.

Once you learn the concept in this book, you will be able to pick up ANY piece of popular music and play it **WITHOUT** needing to read the left hand notes.

I have taught this method in my music classes, to much delight! I have had child and adult students alike who had taken piano lessons for YEARS and still did not know this information, and it has opened up their musical world!

With my method, you will begin to learn how to start playing popular music right away. If you know how to read right-hand piano notes, and know the basics of music, this method is perfect for you! You will be able to play from a popular piano book in no time. Music will begin to MAKE SENSE.

The fun part about learning **Chord Piano** is that you can do so much with it. I would encourage you to pick up any popular music that you like at the music store that has chord symbols, and with the information you learn you will be able to play from one of these books right away! You may also want to pick up a **"Fake Book"**. There are several Fake Books on the market and they show the right hand notes and the chord symbol, much like I have done in this book. See the last chapter of this book, *WHAT NOW,* for more information on Fake Books.

HOW TO USE THIS BOOK

You will be best served with this book if you follow it lesson by lesson, even if you know music. I believe you will find that if you complete the lessons in the order that they are placed, will learn something new. Things that you may have learned in the past will "fall into place" and begin to make real sense. It is "theoretically sound", so that you will be learning universal musical concepts and theory as you go.

If you are interested in purchasing **instructional videos** that go along with each lesson of this book, you can find those at **www.chordpianoisfun.com**.

When playing all of the songs in this book, play the MELODY LINE with your right hand, and the CHORD (noted by "Chord Symbols") with your left hand. You'll learn all about this as you go.

This book is written to teach you **THREE SCALES (KEYS)** in particular – the Keys of C, G, and F (and their Minor cousins). Don't worry if you don't know what this means -- you will learn all about it as you go. After learning these three Keys, you will be able to apply your knowledge to all of music.

The **CHORD STUFF (Addendums)** at the end of the book are meant to be references. These are helpful to refer back to at any stage of your learning process.

At the end of the book, I give several references on what to do after you have finished with **CHORD PIANO IS FUN!**

This book in by no means is an exhaustive composite of all you can learn about playing **Chord Piano**. However, it will give you a very solid, easy to follow start so that you can take off on your own. At the end of this book, I offer other publications that you might want to try after completion.

Thank you again for choosing **CHORD PIANO IS FUN!** I hope it proves to be so for you!

T.K. Goforth
Author
CHORD PIANO IS FUN!
www.chordpianoisfun.com

Instructional Videos that go along with each lesson are available for purchase at **www.chordpianoisfun.com**

Chord Piano Is Fun!

TABLE OF CONTENTS

Chord Piano Is Fun!

LESSONS

NOTES

HOW TO CREATE A MAJOR SCALE
(THE MAJOR SCALE "FORMULA")

What are Scales?

All of music is based on what are called "scales". Scales are the **building blocks** of music. We need **scales** in order to know how to create **chords** (you'll learn about these in Lesson 2). First, however, we need to understand **scales** and know how to BUILD them.

MAJOR SCALES HAVE A "FORMULA"

Let's learn how to "**BUILD**" a Major Scale. We'll start with the "**C Major Scale**" because it is the easiest scale to learn.

Once we do this we will "discover" a **FORMULA** that we can use to create **ANY MAJOR SCALE.**

THE C MAJOR SCALE

The **C Major Scale** is called this because the **first note of the scale is "C".** It is often just called the "**C Scale**". Music that is written with the notes of the **C Major Scale** is called being in the "**Key of C**". You will now begin to "build" your **C Scale** using the diagram of the Treble Staff below:

INSTRUCTIONS:

1.   To draw a C Major Scale on your staff, we start by drawing a whole note on Middle C in the Treble Staff (this has been done for you).

2.	Next, draw a **whole note** on each line and space **up** from Middle C until you get to the next "C" (high C). (Make sure you leave some space between each note you draw and don't draw it directly above the other one). **You should have eight (8) notes on your staff.**

3.	Write the **name of the note** under each note that you have just drawn, starting with "C".

4,	Now, **number** each note by writing "1", "2", "3" etc., above each.

IMPORTANT NOTE: Each note of the scale has a number – called the "**degree**" of the scale. The 1st note (degree) of any scale is called the "**root**" of the scale. The 8th note (degree) of any scale is called an "**octave**".

5.	Now, write out these notes in order and then play them on the piano with your **THUMB (1 finger),** "walking up" the keyboard:

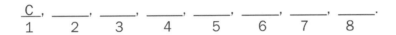

$$\underset{1}{C},\ \underset{2}{\rule{1cm}{0.4pt}},\ \underset{3}{\rule{1cm}{0.4pt}},\ \underset{4}{\rule{1cm}{0.4pt}},\ \underset{5}{\rule{1cm}{0.4pt}},\ \underset{6}{\rule{1cm}{0.4pt}},\ \underset{7}{\rule{1cm}{0.4pt}},\ \underset{8}{\rule{1cm}{0.4pt}}.$$

6.	Next, look at your piano. From Middle C to High C you have both **white notes and black notes**. The space between **each** of these notes is each ½ of a step. So, from Middle C (which is white) to the next note up, (which is black), is **½ step**. Each **two half (1/2) steps** is a **whole step** (½ + ½ = 1).

7.	Notice the "E" note on your piano. Is the next key up a ½ step or a whole step? (Remember, the distance between EACH key on the piano keyboard is ½ step):
_____	The answer should be "½ step".

8.	Notice "B" on your piano. Is the next key up a ½ step or a whole step?
_____	The answer should be "½ step".

9.	Now, play each of the white keys on the piano from Middle C to High C, one at a time. As you go up, write down the distance from one key to the next and note whether this note is a ½ step or a whole step (remember, a whole step is two ½ steps).

Write your answers here (write ½ steps as "H" and whole step as "W"). Example: C to D is a W step.

1. C to D is a _____ step.

2. D to E is a _____ step.

3. E to F is a _____ step.

4. F to G is a _____ step.

5. G to A is a _____ step.

6. A to B is a _____ step.

7. B to C is a _____ step

Do You See A Pattern Above?

The MAJOR SCALE FORMULA is as follows:

W-W-H-W-W-W-H
(Whole Step, Whole Step, Half Step, Whole Step, Whole Step, Whole Step, Half Step)

This formula should be used when building ANY MAJOR SCALE!

Diagram of C Major Scale Shown in Whole Steps and Half Steps:

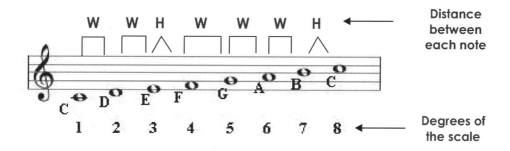

You can also draw the notes on the "Bass Staff". Try this below (the first "C" has been done for you) just so you can see how it looks on the staff. Number and name them as you did with the treble staff.

LESSON 1
HOW TO CREATE A MAJOR SCALE

C MAJOR SCALE PRACTICE

("Key of C" – NO Sharps or Flats)

Music that is written with the notes of the **C Major Scale** is called being in the **"Key of C"**.

NOTE: THE "KEY OF C" HAS NO SHARPS OR FLATS

Practice this scale, using each hand, 10 TIMES EACH HAND (not hands together) using the fingering as shown. You will be crossing fingers over and under. Be sure to SAY THE NOTE NAMES as you play:

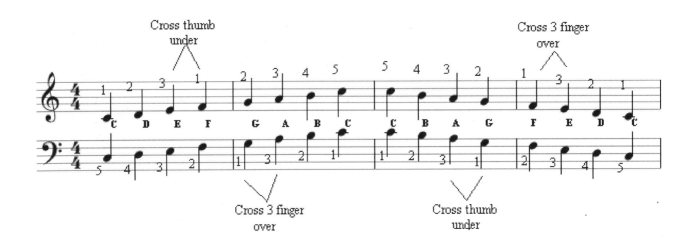

The names of the notes in the **C Major SCALE** are (degrees of the scale are given):

C	D	E	F	G	A	B	C
(1-Root)	(2)	(3)	(4)	(5)	(6)	(7)	(8 - Octave)

← Degrees of the scale

Try practicing the C Major Scale with different rhythms, just for interest. Have fun with it!

HOW TO CREATE A MAJOR CHORD (OR, MAJOR TRIAD)

What is a "Chord"?

A **CHORD** is two or more notes played together at the same time.
A **TRIAD** is a three-note chord made up of a particular formula (more on this later!)

Once you understand chords, you will begin to see how music is made up. You will also be able to play songs that are written with "lead sheets" or "chord charts". This is very valuable if you want to play popular music.

BUILDING A MAJOR TRIAD/CHORD USING THE "C CHORD"

We are going to learn to "build" a **MAJOR TRIAD** (also known as a **MAJOR CHORD**), which is the most common type of chord and the chord from which other chords are made. A Major Triad consists of **three** notes. We will first build the "**C Major Triad**" (which is called the "**C Major Chord**") because it is the easiest to learn and is the **ROOT** note of the **C Scale**.

Review:

Here is a review of the scale you drew in *Lesson 1 - How To Create A Major Scale*. Remember that you numbered each note with a number between 1 and 8:

<u>C</u>	<u>D</u>	<u>E</u>	<u>F</u>	<u>G</u>	<u>A</u>	<u>B</u>	<u>C</u>	← Degrees of the scale
(**1**- Root)	(**2**)	(**3**)	(**4**)	(**5**)	(**6**)	(**7**)	(**8**	
							Octave**)**	

(**Remember:** Each note of the scale has a number – called the "**degree**" of the scale. The **1st note** (degree) of any scale is called the "**root**" of the scale. The **8th note** (degree) of any scale is called an "octave". *The NAME of any scale is based upon the "<u>root</u>" of the scale.*)

M3 + m3

NOW, WE WILL FIND THE MAJOR CHORD/TRIAD* FORMULA

Again, the names of the notes in the **C Major Scale** are:

C	D	E	F	G	A	B	C
(1-Root)	(2)	(3)	(4)	(5)	(6)	(7)	(8 - ← Degrees of the scale
							Octave)

TO FIND THE C MAJOR CHORD (TRIAD*):

Name the **1st, 3rd, and 5th** degrees of the C Major Scale above:

_____,   _____, and   _____.
(1st - "Root")   (3rd)   (5th)

THAT'S IT! THIS IS HOW YOU CREATE A MAJOR CHORD KNOWN AS THE MAJOR TRIAD*!

To create a **MAJOR CHORD (TRIAD*) FORMULA**
YOU NEED TO LOCATE THE
1st, 3rd, AND 5th DEGREES OF THE SCALE!

This is the way to find ANY OTHER MAJOR CHORD (TRIAD*).

*Note: A **triad** is always a **chord**, but a **chord** is **not always** a triad. We will learn more about other chords as we go. However, in the course of this book, I will be referring to the **MAJOR TRIAD** as the **MAJOR CHORD**, which is made up of the **1st, 3rd, and 5th** degrees of a scale.

DRAWING THE C MAJOR CHORD

These three notes (C, E, and G) make up the <u>**C Major Chord,**</u> **which we will just refer to as the "C CHORD".** (It is also called the <u>**"C Major Triad".**</u>) Draw them on this staff using **whole notes.** (It should look like a snowman.) Once you are finished, play them on the piano using the **1, 3, and 5 fingers** of the **right** hand. (Check your work on next page).

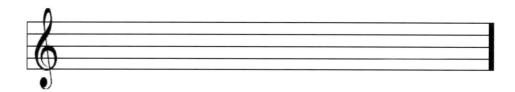

Now do the same on the Bass Clef and play this as well and play the chord with your **5, 3, and 1 fingers** of the left hand. (Check your work on next page).

CHORD PRACTICE TECHNIQUE #1

BLOCK CHORD

RIGHT HAND

This is what the C chord looks like on the staff at Middle C:

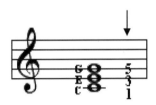

Play this chord at each octave of the piano, starting from the lowest "C". **SAY THE NOTE NAMES AS YOU PLAY.**

LEFT HAND

This is what the C chord looks like on the staff at Bass C:

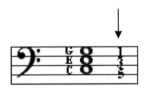

Play this chord at each octave of the piano, starting from the lowest "C". **SAY THE NOTE NAMES AS YOU PLAY.**

CHORD PRACTICE TECHNIQUE #2

BROKEN CHORD

RIGHT HAND

Break the C chord up by playing "C-E-G-Chord", starting from the lowest "C" of the piano .
(Be sure to always use the same fingering for the chords: <u>1-3-5 fingers for the right hand</u>.)
SAY THE NOTE NAMES AS YOU PLAY.

This is how it looks on the staff at Middle C:

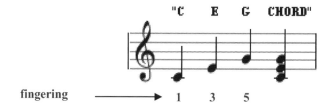

fingering ⟶ 1   3   5

LEFT HAND

Repeat the same as with the left hand. (Be sure to always use the same fingering for the
chords: <u>5-3-1 for the left hand</u>.) **SAY THE NOTE NAMES AS YOU PLAY.**

This is how it looks on the staff at Bass C:

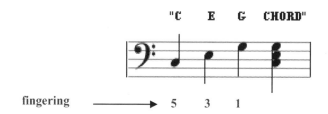

fingering ⟶ 5   3   1

CHORD PRACTICE TECHNIQUE #3

ARPEGGIO

An "**arpeggio**" is actually just a **broken chord**. We are going to practice it in a fun, very dramatic way. In this exercise, you will be using **both hands**. (**PLEASE read carefully, and you'll get it! Don't let this page scare you!**)

TECHNIQUE:

1. Place your <u>**left hand 5 finger**</u> (pinky finger) **on the LOWEST C of the keyboard**. Find the **C chord** (C-E-G) in this location with correct fingering.

2. Then, place your **right hand** at the **very next octave**, and put your **1 finger** (thumb) **on that C** and find that C Chord.

3. Play the chords as **broken chords** up the piano, left hand then right hand, **crossing left hand over right as you go**.

4. Repeat this process all the way up the keyboard and **at the very last octave end with just the C note with your left hand crossed over the right**.

DIAGRAM:

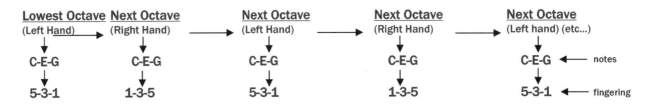

Lowest Octave (Left Hand)	Next Octave (Right Hand)	Next Octave (Left Hand)	Next Octave (Right Hand)	Next Octave (Left hand) (etc...)	
↓	↓	↓	↓	↓	
C-E-G	C-E-G	C-E-G	C-E-G	C-E-G	← notes
↓	↓	↓	↓	↓	
5-3-1	1-3-5	5-3-1	1-3-5	5-3-1	← fingering

Practice this until you can play it quickly, one hand after the other. When you feel comfortable, use the **pedal** and hold it down while you are playing the entire arpeggio.

NOTE: IF YOU CANNOT REACH THE BOTTOM OF THE PIANO WHILE SITTING, BEGIN AT THE LOWEST OCTAVE YOU CAN REACH, GOING UP TO THE HIGHEST OCTAVE YOU CAN REACH.

Last One RH

C E G C

1 2 3 5

End
5/20/19

HOW TO BUILD THE G MAJOR SCALE AND G CHORD

As you recall from *Lesson 1,* creating a Major Scale requires a certain **FORMULA.**

> This formula is: **W-W-H-W-W-W-H**

Follow the steps to build a C Major scale, using the same **W-W-H-W-W-W-H** pattern, **and you will be able to build ANY OTHER Major Scale**. In this lesson we will build the **G Major Scale and find the G Chord.**

BUILDING THE G MAJOR SCALE

Music that is written with the notes of the **G Major Scale** is called being in the **"Key of G"**.

On your piano, play the G above Middle C. From the **pattern** we learned in Lesson 1 of **Whole Steps and Half Steps (W-W-H-W-W-W-H)**, write down the next note in this pattern: For example, the note that is a W (whole step) after G is A (the first one and a half are done for you):

<u>G</u> to <u>A</u> is a <u>W</u> step
<u>A</u> to <u>B</u> is a <u>W</u> step
____ to C is a <u>H</u> step
____ to D is a <u>W</u> step
____ to E is a <u>W</u> step
____ to F# is a <u>W</u> step
____ to G is a <u>H</u> step

2. Did you notice that one of these notes is not on a white key, but is on a black key? This key is called "F#" or "F sharp". (The reason it is called "F sharp" and not "G flat" is because scales need to be in "alphabetical order".)

3. Write out these notes in order: _G_ , ____, _____, _____, _____, _____, _____, _____.

                       1   2   3   4   5   6   7   8

NOTE: THE "KEY OF G" HAS 1 SHARP: F#

HELPFUL NOTE: A "sharp" is when you go to the **VERY NEXT NOTE (white or black)** to the **RIGHT** of the key that is named (or **UP** the piano keyboard). For example, if the note is **F** Sharp, you find the F and go <u>UP the piano keyboard ½ step.</u> Think if when you sit on something SHARP – you jump **UP!** When you SHARP a note you move ½ step **UP** the keyboard.

4. Now, write the notes of the G Major Scale out on the following staffs **with whole notes.** (For ease in practice sake, be sure to put a **# (sharp)** sign to the **left** of the note you write on "F".)

Tip: From the lowest "G" on the scale (since this is the G Major Scale), **draw a whole note on EACH LINE AND EACH SPACE UNTIL YOU HAVE 8 NOTES DRAWN OUT.** Then add the sharps to the left of each "F". This is how you draw out **ALL** Major Scales.

Key Signatures
(you will find out
about these in
Lessons 10 and 11)

FINDING THE G CHORD

Review of the G Scale:

The names of the notes in the G Major SCALE are (degrees of the scale are given):

<u>G</u>	<u>A</u>	<u>B</u>	<u>C</u>	<u>D</u>	<u>E</u>	<u>F#</u>	<u>G</u>	
(1-Root)	(2)	(3)	(4)	(5)	(6)	(7)	(8 - Octave)	← Degrees of the scale

Remember:

The **MAJOR CHORD FORMULA** IS TO FIND THE

<u>1</u>st, <u>3</u>rd, AND <u>5</u>th DEGREES OF THE SCALE!

Now, use the above **MAJOR CHORD FORMULA** and the **G Scale** to find the **G Chord**:

_____, _____, and _____.
(1st - Root) (3rd)   (5th).

You should have come up with:

<u>G,</u>   <u>B,</u> **and** <u>D.</u>
(1st- Root) (3rd)   (5th).

These three notes make up the **G Chord**. Draw them on these staffs using whole notes. For the G in the Bass Clef, start on the Low G line. (They should look like snowmen.)

LESSON 3
HOW TO BUILD THE G MAJOR SCALE
AND G CHORD

G MAJOR SCALE PRACTICE
("Key of G" -- 1 Sharp: F#)

Practice the G Major Scale with each hand. **SAY THE NOTE NAMES AS YOU PLAY**. Play it 10 times each hand before moving on to the other hand. Try practicing it with different rhythms just for interest.

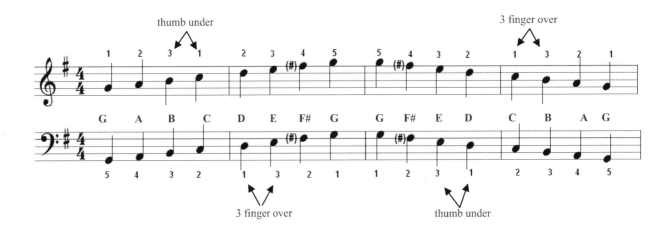

G MAJOR CHORD PRACTICE

The names of the notes in the G Major Chord are:

G   B   D

Practice the G Major Chord using the three practice techniques in **Lesson 2 - How to Create a Major Chord:**

- Practice Technique # 1: Chord Practice
- Practice Technique # 2: Broken Chord Practice
- Practice Technique # 3: Arpeggio Practice

TIME TO PLAY YOUR FIRST SONG WITH "CHORD CHARTS"!

Try these songs using the **C Chord** and the **G Chord**! The following two songs are written with **"chord symbols"** above the written music. This type of music is considered a **"chord chart"** or a **"lead sheet"** – it shows the harmony of the song given as a **chord symbol** rather than as written notes.

In these songs, you are going to be playing the **melody with your right hand**, and the **harmony (chord) with your left hand**. Notice the **"C"** and **"G"** above the staff and above certain notes. These are the new chords (C and G) that you have learned.

Instructions:

1. To begin, first practice the song with your **right hand** until you can easily play the **melody**.

2. Then, practice moving between the C and G Chord with your left hand. These chords will be the **harmony**. Play the **C** Chord (C-E-G) **starting at Bass C** (the C below middle C) and play the **G** Chord (G-B-D) starting **at the G BELOW Bass C**. When you feel comfortable with both, put them together as the next step:

3. **Play each chord as a BLOCK CHORD at the same time you play the note in the melody that it is written directly below the chord symbol.** You can just hold the chord until it is time to change to the next chord. Or, you can play the chord again until the next chord shows up. Give it a try! It's **FUN!**

MARY HAD A LITTLE LAMB
C and G Chords

C Chord played as "C-E-G"
G Chord played as "G-B-D"

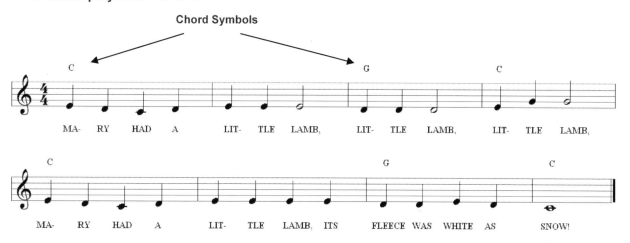

POP GOES THE WEASEL
C and G Chords

C Chord played as "C-E-G"
G Chord played as "G-B-D"

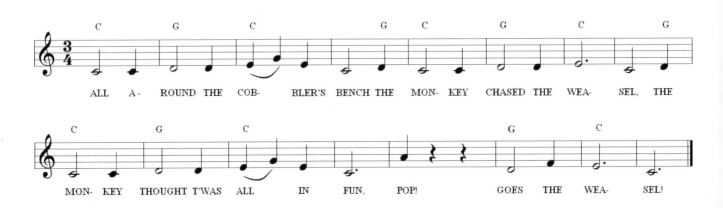

CONGRATULATIONS ON PLAYING YOUR FIRST SONGS WITH CHORD CHARTS!

HOW TO BUILD THE F MAJOR SCALE
AND F CHORD

As you recall from *Lesson 1*, the **MAJOR SCALE FORMULA** is:

(W-W-H-W-W-W-H)

(Whole Step, Whole Step, Half Step, Whole Step, Whole Step, Whole Step, Half Step)

BUILDING THE F MAJOR SCALE

Music that is written with the notes of the **F Major Scale** is called being in the **"Key of F"**.

On your piano, play the F above Middle C. Use the **MAJOR SCALE FORMULA** to find the notes in the **F MAJOR SCALE**. (The first one and a half are done for you):

__F__ to __G__ is a __W__ step

__G__ to _____ is a __W__ step

_____ to _____ is a __H__ step

_____ to _____ is a __W__ step

_____ to _____ is a __W__ step

_____ to _____ is a __W__ step

_____ to _____ is a __H__ step

2. Did you notice that one of these notes is not on a white key, but is on a black key? This key is called "B♭" or "B Flat".

3. Write out these notes in order: __F__, ____, ____, _____, _____, _____, _____, _____.
                                     1   2   3   4   5   6   7   8

NOTE: THE "KEY OF F" HAS 1 FLAT: B$^\flat$

HELPFUL NOTE: A "flat" is when you go to the VERY NEXT NOTE (white or black) to the **LEFT** (or **DOWN** the keyboard) from the key that is named. For example, if the note is B Flat, you find the B and go ½ step **DOWN** the piano keyboard). Think of a FLAT TIRE. When the tire is FLAT, it goes **DOWN**. When you FLAT a note, you go ½ **step DOWN** the keyboard.

4. Now, write the notes of the F Major Scale out on the following staffs with **whole notes**. Be sure to put a $\flat$ sign to the left of the note you write on "F". **Tip:** From the lowest "F" on the scale (since this is the F Major Scale), **draw a whole note on EACH LINE AND EACH SPACE UNTIL YOU HAVE 8 NOTES DRAWN OUT.** Then add the flats to the left of each "B". This is how you draw out **ALL** Major Scales.

Key Signatures
(you will find out
about these in
Lessons 10 and 11)

FINDING THE F CHORD

Review of the F Scale:

The names of the notes in the **F Major SCALE** are (degrees of the scale are given):

F	G	A	B♭	C	D	E	F
(1- Root)	(2)	(3)	(4)	(5)	(6)	(7)	(8 – Octave - same as root)

Remember:

> The **MAJOR CHORD FORMULA** IS TO FIND THE
>
> <u>1st</u>, <u>3rd</u>, AND <u>5th</u> DEGREES OF THE SCALE!

Now, use the above **MAJOR CHORD FORMULA** and the **F Scale** to find the **F Chord**:

_____, _____, and _____.
(1st - Root)　　　(3rd)　　　　(5th)

You should have come up with:

<u>F,</u>　　<u>A,</u>　　and　　<u>C.</u>
(1st　　　(3rd)　　　　　(5th).
Root)

These three notes make up the **F Chord**.

Draw them on these staffs using whole notes. (They should look like snowmen.)

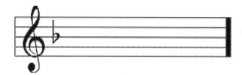 

F MAJOR SCALE PRACTICE
("Key of F" - 1 FLAT: B♭)

Practice the F Major Scale with each hand. **SAY THE NOTE NAMES AS YOU PLAY.** Play it 10 times each hand before moving on to the other hand. Try practicing it with different rhythms just for interest.

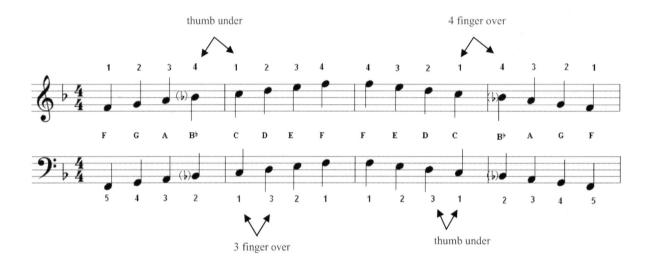

F MAJOR CHORD PRACTICE

The names of the notes in the F Major Chord are:

F   A   C

Practice the F Major Chord using the three Practice Techniques in *Lesson 2 - How to Create a Major Chord*:

- Practice Technique # 1: Block Chord Practice
- Practice Technique # 2: Broken / Block Chord Practice
- Practice Technique # 3: Arpeggio Practice

MORE ABOUT SCALES

We've already discovered that each note of each scale has a certain number, or "degree". In addition, these "degrees" are also called different things, or notated in different ways in music. This lesson shows these additional names or notations.

SCALE DEGREE NAMES ("Technical Names")

As you remember from *Lesson 1*, each note of the scale has a certain number, or **degree**.

In addition to the numbers, the **degrees of the scale** have **TECHNICAL NAMES**. These are based on the way that they "sound". This goes into a lot of music information (theory) that I won't cover here right now. But for now, here are the **NAMES (Technical Names)** for each of the degrees of the scale. Here is the C Major Scale with both its **NUMBERS** and **NAMES**:

C MAJOR SCALE

C	D	E	F	G	A	B	C
(1 – Root)	(2)	(3)	(4)	(5)	(6)	(7)	(8 – Octave - same as root)
Tonic	Supertonic	Mediant	Sub-dominant	Dominant	Submediant	Leading Tone	Tonic

You will see these **NAMES** throughout your life in music, and you will want to be familiar with them. You may also want to do your own research into **why** the technical names of the degrees of the scale are called this, but right now we will just make sure you are familiar with their names.

Chord Piano Is Fun

WORKSHEET

1. What is the **Technical Name** for the **6th** degree of a scale? _____

2. What **note** is the **1st** degree of the scale in the C Major Scale? _____

3. What **degree** of the scale is the **Supertonic**? _____

4. What **note** is the **Submediant** in the C Major Scale? _____

5. What is the **Technical Name** for the **4th** degree of the scale? _____

6. What **degree** of the scale is the **Leading Tone**? _____

7. What is the **Technical Name** for the **3rd** degree of the scale? _____

8. a. What **note** is the **5th** degree of the C Major Scale? _____

    b. What is its **Technical Name**? _____

ANSWERS FOR LESSON 5 WORKSHEET:

1. Submediant

2. C

3. 2

4. A

5. Sub-dominant

6. 7

7. Mediant

8. a. G
   b. Dominant

NOTES

SCALES, KEYS, AND THEIR CHORDS
(FAMILY CHORDS)

What are "Family Chords"?

FAMILY CHORDS are the chords in each Scale (or, "Key") that show up more often in songs written in that key more than any other.

HOW DO I FIND THE FAMILY CHORDS?

As you recall from *Lesson 1 – How to Create Major Scale* and *Lesson 5 – More About Scales*, each note of the scale has a number (or degree) and these also have **Technical Names**.

Review of the C Major Scale:

	<u>C</u>	D	E	F	G	A	B	<u>C</u>
Degrees of the scale →	(1- Root)	(2)	(3)	(4)	(5)	(6)	(7)	(8 – Octave (same as root)
Technical Name →	Tonic	Supertonic	Mediant	Sub-dominant	Dominant	Submediant	Leading Tone	Tonic

**From EACH ONE of these notes (the degrees of the scale)
we can create TRIADS.**

A **TRIAD** is a **three-note CHORD** made up from the
1st, 3rd , and 5th degrees of a particular scale.

In this lesson, we will be using the word "**TRIAD**" interchangeably
with the word "**Chord**" (see *Lesson 2 – How to Create a Major Chord*).

Chord Piano Is Fun!

Instructions:

1. Starting on the C of the C scale, with your right hand play the "C Chord" (C Triad) with your 1-3-5 fingers (use the **BLOCK CHORD**).

2. Now, play a **TRIAD** on **each note of the C Scale**, using your 1, 3 and 5 fingers in the same form as you did for the C Chord. In other words, just "walk up" the keyboard, keeping your hand in the same position, playing **TRIADS** all the way up the C Scale, one after the other starting on C —play a triad starting on C, then starting on D, then starting on E, etc. up to the next octave C. (In other words, create a triad from each note of the scale.)

Here is how it would look on the treble staff with your right hand:

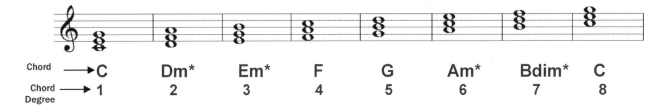

Chord ➡	C	Dm*	Em*	F	G	Am*	Bdim*	C
Chord Degree ➡	1	2	3	4	5	6	7	8

Do the same with your left hand, using the **5-3-1 fingers** of your left hand and starting on Bass C rather than Middle C.

All of the above TRIADS/CHORDS are considered **FAMILY CHORDS** in the Key of C, and will show up in many songs written in the Key of C! Now you know!

NOTE NAME "ADDITIONS"

From the above diagram, you will notice that some notes have "additions" such as "m" or "dim" written after them (as in "Dm", and also "dim", such as "Bdim"). This means that they are different "types" of Chords rather than a **Major** Chord. These chords could be **Minor (m)** or **Diminished (dim)**.

This will be explained on **Page 31 – Types of Chords**!

ROMAN NUMERAL NOTATIONS

As with scales, chords also have more than one name for each chord. These are the **Chord Degree** and the **Technical Name**). In addition to **the Chord Degree**, and the **Technical Name**, chords (triads) also have **Roman Numeral Notations**.

For example, the **I** Chord (1st Chord) in the Key of C is the **C Chord**, the **IV** Chord (4th Chord) is the **F Chord,** etc.

You will notice below that each of the chords has a **ROMAN NUMERAL** below it:

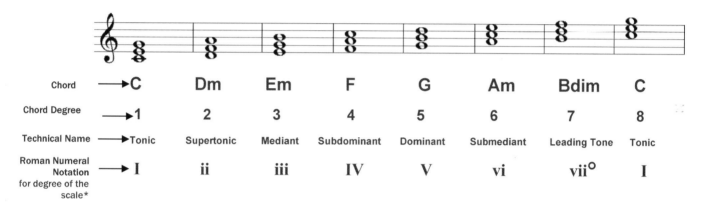

Chord	C	Dm	Em	F	G	Am	Bdim	C
Chord Degree	1	2	3	4	5	6	7	8
Technical Name	Tonic	Supertonic	Mediant	Subdominant	Dominant	Submediant	Leading Tone	Tonic
Roman Numeral Notation for degree of the scale*	I	ii	iii	IV	V	vi	vii°	I

* TYPE of chord shown by upper or lower case letters. See below.

Note: You would **say** these Roman Numerals the same way you would say the usual numbering (i.e., "I" is "one" "ii" is "two", etc.)

> The above **ROMAN NUMERAL NOTATIONS** are used for **the MAJOR SCALE.**
> The **ROMAN NUMERAL NOTATION** tells us
> what **TYPE** of chord/triad you will be playing.

Let me explain:

Take a look at the **Roman Numeral** under the scale. You will notice that some of the Roman Numerals are in **UPPER CASE** and some of them are in **LOWER CASE**. This is very important. Like the notations afterward ("**m**" or "**dim**"), these "cases" tell us **WHAT TYPE** of Triad/Chord these will be -- either **Major**, **Minor**, or **Diminished**.

This will be explained on **Page 31 – Types of Chords!**

TYPES OF CHORDS

Types of Chords are distinguished by their **SOUND QUALITY**. This means, that a Major Chord sounds different than a Minor Chord, and a Diminished chord has an altogether different sound. As you practice playing these types of chords, (which will be discussed more in detail later), you will become used to their sound and may be able to pick out a Minor Chord from a Major Chord or Diminished Chord.

A Major Chord is notated with just the name of the Chord (such as **C**, **F, or G**). There is no need to add the word "Major" after the name. Major Chords sound "**happy**". We've already discovered how to find or "create" Major Chords from Major Scales in **Lesson 2 - How To Create Major Chord**. *A Major Chord is indicated by the UPPER CASE Roman Numeral.*

A Minor Chord is notated with the name of the Chord, but with the addition of an "**m**" or "**-**" behind it (i.e., **Dm** or **Am**, or can also be written as **D-** or **A-**). Minor Chords sound "**sad**". You will find out how to create Minor Chords in **Lesson 9 – The Twelve Major and Minor Chords**. *A Minor Chord is indicated the by the LOWER CASE Roman Numeral.*

A Diminished Chord is notated with the name of the Chord, but with the addition of the letters "dim" or the symbol "°" behind it (i.e. **Bdim**, or can also be written as **B°**). Diminished Chords sound "**tense**" or "**scary**". You will find out how to create Diminished Chords in **Lesson 24 – Building Other Types of Chords**. *A Diminished Chord is indicated by a LOWER CASE Roman Numeral plus the "°" symbol behind it.*

All In Review

Here are all the names and notations of the scale degrees used in music (**based on the Key of C**):

	C	Dm	Em	F	G	Am	Bdim	C
Chord Degrees	(1- Root)	(2)	(3)	(4)	(5)	(6)	(7)	(8 – Octave (same as root)
Roman Numeral Notation	I	ii	iii	IV	V	vi	vii°	I
Technical Name	Tonic	Supertonic	Mediant	Sub-dominant	Dominant	Submediant	Leading Tone	Tonic

WORKSHEET (refer to previous 2 pages)

1. What is the **Technical Name** for the **5th** triad of a scale? _____

2. What is the **Roman Numeral Notation** for the **6th** triad of the Major Scale? _____

3. What chord is the **Submediant** chord in the Key of C? _____

4. What is the **Supertonic** chord in the Key of C? _____

5. What **type** of chord (**Major, Minor, or Diminished**) is the **6 chord** in the Major Scale? _____

6. What is the **Roman Numeral Notation** for the **Mediant** triad of the Major Scale? _____

7. What is the **Technical Name** for the **4th** triad of the scale? _____

8. What is the **Roman Numeral Notation** for the **3rd** triad of the Major Scale? _____

9. What **type** of chord (**Major, Minor, or Diminished**) is the **7 chord** in the Major Scale? _____

10. a. What is the **Leading Tone** chord in the Key of C? _____.

    b. What is its **Roman Numeral Notation**? _____

11. What is the **Roman Numeral Notation** for the **2nd** degree of the Major Scale? _____

12. What is the **Technical Name** for the **1st** degree of the scale? _____

13. a. What is the **5th chord** in the Key of C? _____

    b. What is its **Roman Numeral Notation**? _____

    c. What is its **Technical Name**? _____

14. What **type** of chord is the **4 chord** in the Major Scale? _____

ANSWERS FOR LESSON 6 WORKSHEET

1.   **Dominant**

2.   **vi**

3.   **Am**

4.   **Dm**

5.   **Minor**

6.   **iii**

7.   **Subdominant**

8.   **iii**

9.   **Diminished**

10.   **a. Bdim**
       b. vii°

11.   **ii**

12.   **Tonic**

13.   **a. G**
       b. V
       c. Dominant

14.   **Major**

THE THREE MOST IMPORTANT FAMILY CHORDS

As you remember from your *Lesson 6 – Scales and their Chords*, each scale has certain **FAMILY CHORDS** which are chords that belong in a certain "key" or a certain scale. For example, if you are playing a song in the "Key of C", you would be using the notes in the "C Scale". In addition, you would be most likely using the "FAMILY CHORDS" belonging to the C Scale.

Family Chords are built from each note of the scale. Just as with the notes of the scale, each CHORD (triad) of the scale also has a certain degree (number) and **Roman Numeral** notation.

Here is a review of the C Major Scale Family Chords:

	C	Dm	Em	F	G	Am	Bdim	C	← Triad built on notes of the scale.
Roman Numeral Notation →	I	ii	iii	IV	V	vi	vii°	I	← Chord Degrees
	1	2	3	4	5	6	7	8	

Within these **FAMILY CHORDS,** there are **THREE** in particular that are the **MOST IMPORTANT**. These three chords show up more often than any other chords in any song. By knowing **these three most important family chords of each key**, you will be able to play many, many songs!

The **THREE MOST IMPORTANT CHORDS** are:

The I Chord, the IV Chord, and the V Chord
(Roman Numeral Notation).

FINDING THE THREE MOST IMPORTANT FAMILY CHORDS

As stated on the previous page, the **THREE MOST IMPORTANT FAMILY CHORDS** are the
I (1st), **IV** (4th) and **V** (5th) chords (triads) of each scale. We are going to find these chords
in the C Major Scale.

REVIEW OF C MAJOR SCALE:

	C	Dm	Em	F	G	Am	Bdim	C ←	Triad built on notes of the scale.
Roman Numeral Notation →	I	ii	iii	IV	V	vi	vii°	I	
	1	2	3	4	5	6	7	8 ←	Chord Degrees

INSTRUCTIONS:

From the above chart, which chord would be the "**I**" (**or 1**) chord in the **C Major Scale**?

_____ Chord

Which chord would be the "**IV**" (**or 4**) chord in the **C Major Scale**?

_____ Chord

Which chord would be the "**V**" (**or 5**) chord in the **C Major Scale**?

_____ Chord

So, the **THREE MOST IMPORTANT CHORDS**
in the **C Major Scale** are:

C	F	G
I	IV	V
(1)	(4)	(5)

PRACTICE IN THE KEY OF C
(C MAJOR SCALE)

Right now we are going to use the **THREE MOST IMPORTANT** family chords in the **Key of C** (based on the C Major Scale) because it is the easiest key to work in.

You've already learned the **C Chord** (I chord), **F Chord** (IV chord), and **G Chord** (V Chord) in previous lessons and even learned a few songs with both the C Chord and G chord. Now we are going to learn a few songs that include the F Chord.

With the left hand, practice moving between **the C, F, and G Chords** until you can do it smoothly. These chords will be the **harmony**. Play the C Chord (C-E-G) **starting at Bass C** (the C below middle C), play the **G** Chord (G-B-D) **starting at the G <u>below</u> Bass C**, and also play the **F** Chord (F-A-C) **starting at the F <u>below</u> Bass C**. When you feel comfortable with both, put them together as the next step:

For each song, practice the melody with the right hand until you can play it easily.

<u>C</u>, <u>F</u>, <u>G</u>, Chords
(I, IV, V Chords)

YANKEE DOODLE

(written in the Key of C – no sharps or flats)
C, F and G Chords (I, IV and V Chords)

C Chord (I Chord) played as "C-E-G"
F Chord (IV Chord) played as "F-A-C"
G Chord (V Chord) played as "G-B-D

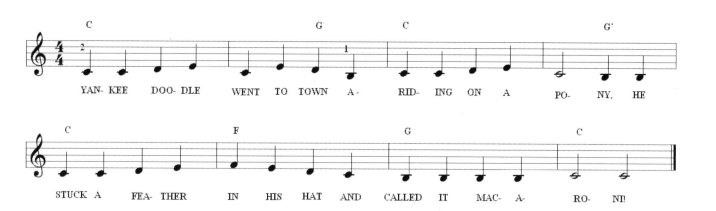

TWINKLE, TWINKLE LITTLE STAR

(written in the Key of C – no sharps or flats)
C, F and G Chords (I, IV and V Chords)

C Chord (I Chord) played as "C-E-G"
F Chord (IV Chord) played as "F-A-C"
G Chord (V Chord) played as "G-B-D"

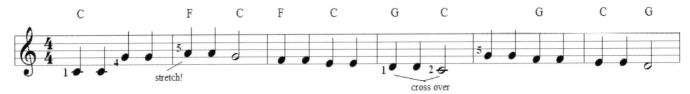

JINGLE BELLS

(written in the Key of C – no sharps or flats)
C, F and G Chords (I, IV and V Chords)

C Chord (I Chord) played as "C-E-G"
F Chord (IV Chord) played as "F-A-C"
G Chord (V Chord) played as "G-B-D"

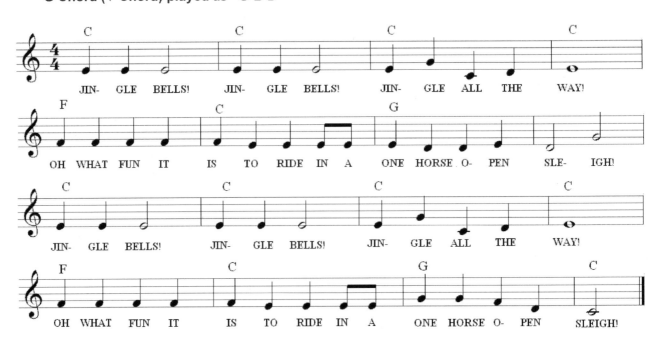

CHORD INVERSIONS

What is a Chord Inversion?

A "**CHORD INVERSION**" is what you call a chord when the notes are played "out of order".

In other words, if you have the **G Chord**, which consists of **G-B-D,** you do not always have to play the notes with the **G** on the bottom, the **B** in the middle, and the **D** on the top. You can mix them up! We do this so that it is easier to move from one chord to another.

Instructions:

For example, take a look at the songs in *Lesson 7* – especially "**Twinkle, Twinkle**". I'm sure you've discovered that it is quite awkward to jump so quickly from the C Chord, to the F Chord, and to the G Chord. To make this easier, this is what we do:

- Name the notes in the C Chord: **C E G**

- Name the notes in the G Chord: **G B D**

- Name the notes in the F Chord: **F A C**

- With your **LEFT HAND**, play the **C Chord as usual with the C at the bottom (5-3-1 fingers).**

- Now, before moving to the G Chord, can you see if there is any note in the G Chord that is also in the C Chord? If yes, what note is it? _____

So, what you would do after playing the C Chord is to leave your 1 finger on the "G" and move the 5 finger DOWN to the "B" and the 3 finger DOWN to the "D". So, instead of playing **G B D**, you will play <u>**B D G**</u>, but those notes are all in the G Chord, so it works!

Try to see how you would do this with the F Chord. Is there a note that is in both the C Chord and the F Chord? _____

In what order would you play the notes of this chord after playing the C Chord to make it easier to move to?   ____ _____ ____

PRACTICE #1
INVERSION PRACTICE

You are going to practice moving back and forth between each inversion, so that it will become easier for you.

INSTRUCTIONS:

LEFT HAND (Be sure to follow using the **fingering** noted):

We are using our left hand first because in this book we will be mostly playing the chords with our left hand. Be sure to follow using the **fingering** noted:

- Start with the left hand with the **C Chord** in **ROOT POSITION:**   **C E G** (5-3-1 fingers)

- Then, move to the **F Chord INVERSION** (2nd Inversion*):   **C F A** (5-2-1 fingers)

- Then, move to the **G Chord 1st INVERSION** (1st Inversion*):   **B D G** (5-3-1 fingers)

- Then move back to the **C Chord** in **ROOT POSITION:**   **C E G** (5-3-1 fingers)

- Do this several times, until it becomes easy.

RIGHT HAND (Be sure to follow using the **fingering** noted):

- Start with the right hand with the C **Chord** in **ROOT POSITION:**   **C E G** (1-3-5 fingers)

- Then, move to the **F Chord INVERSION** (2nd Inversion*):   **C F A** (1-3-5 fingers)

- Then, move to the **G Chord INVERSION** (1st Inversion*):   **B D G** (1-2-5 fingers)

- Then move back to the **C Chord** in **ROOT POSITION:**   **C E G** (1-3-5 fingers)

- Do this several times, until it becomes easy.

- Then, go on to the next practice, "Chord Chart Practice."

*NOTE: **Types** of inversions are discussed and illustrated on last page of this lesson.

PRACTICE #2
CHORD CHART PRACTICE

Try playing the following songs with **INVERSIONS**:

MARY HAD A LITTLE LAMB

(written in the Key of C – no sharps or flats)
C and G Chords (I and V Chords)

C Chord (I Chord) played as "C-E-G"
G Chord (V Chord) played as "B-D-G" (1st Inversion*)

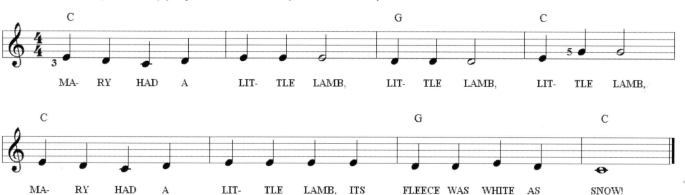

POP GOES THE WEASEL

(written in the Key of C – no sharps or flats)
C and G Chords (I and V Chords)

C Chord (I Chord) played as "C-E-G"
G Chord (V Chord) played as "B-D-G" (1st Inversion*)

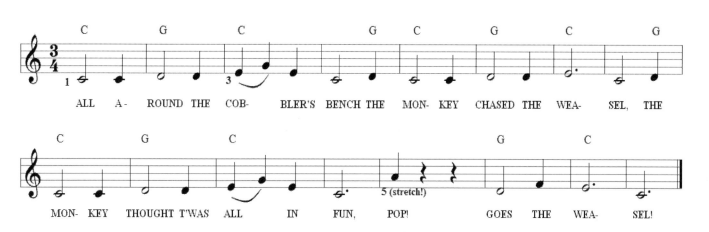

LESSON 8
CHORD INVERSIONS AND PRACTICE

Chord Piano Is Fun!

YANKEE DOODLE

(written in the Key of C – no sharps or flats)
C, F and G Chords (I, IV and V Chords)

C Chord (I Chord) played as "C-E-G"
F Chord (IV Chord) played as "C-F-A" (2nd Inversion)
G Chord (V Chord) played as "B-D-G" (1st Inversion)

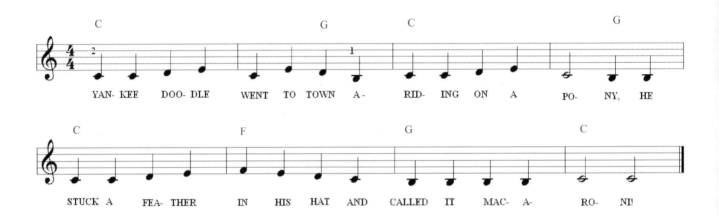

TWINKLE, TWINKLE LITTLE STAR

(written in the Key of C – no sharps or flats)
C, F and G Chords (I, IV and V Chords)

C Chord (I Chord) played as "C-E-G"
F Chord (IV Chord) played as "C-F-A" (2nd Inversion)
G Chord (V Chord) played as "B-D-G" (1st Inversion)

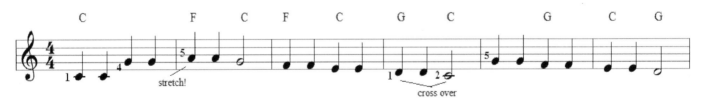

JINGLE BELLS

(written in the Key of C – no sharps or flats)
C, F and G Chords (I, IV and V Chords)

C Chord (I Chord) played as "C-E-G"
F Chord (IV Chord) played as "C-F-A" (2nd Inversion)
G Chord (V Chord) played as "B-D-G" (1st Inversion)

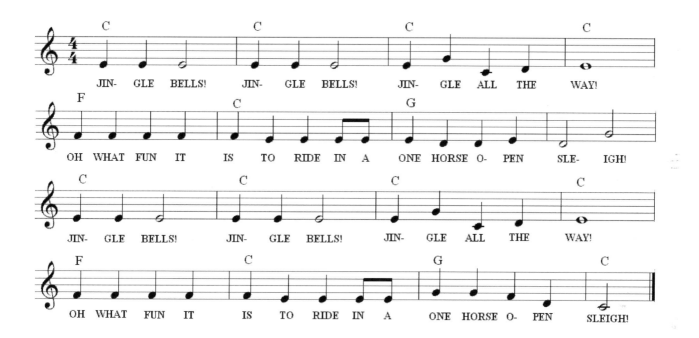

TYPES OF INVERSIONS

As stated, chords that are "mixed up" are called "inversions". Here are the **types** of inversions (based on the C Chord):

ROOT POSITION:

If you play a chord with the ROOT at the bottom (i.e., **C** E G), this is called being in the **ROOT POSITION.**

Example: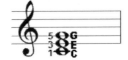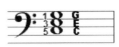

FIRST INVERSION:

If you play the chord by moving the C to the end of the chord (E G **C**), this is called the **FIRST INVERSION**. (You used the "First Inversion" of the **G Chord** in your **Inversion Practice** and **Chord Chart Songs** above.)

Example: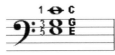

SECOND INVERSION:

If you play the chord by moving the C to the middle (G **C** E) this is called the **SECOND INVERSION**. (You used the "Second Inversion" of **the F Chord** in your **Inversion Practice** and **Chord Chart Songs** above.)

Example:

"SLASH CHORDS":

This is an example of what is called a "**Slash Chord**": C/E. This means that they want you to play the **C Chord** but with the **E as the bottom (lowest) note.**

THE TWELVE MAJOR and MINOR CHORDS (TRIADS)

You have now learned that in ANY key, there are **THREE MOST IMPORTANT CHORDS**. You have also learned, specifically, the **THREE MOST IMPORTANT** chords which belong in the Key of C.

This lesson is probably the most important lesson in this book. You are now going to learn to play **ALL TWELVE MAJOR CHORDS** so that you will be able to find them quickly. Once you know all of these chords, you will be able to play hundreds of songs, and will become invaluable once you know which THREE **MOST IMPORTANT CHORDS** belong in each Key.

Major Chords are the chords from which all other chords are made. Once you know Major Chords, finding any other type of chord will be a snap. As you recall from **Lesson 6 – Scales and Their Chords,** Major Chords have a certain sound, which makes them sound "happy".

Besides being able to be created as we did in **Lesson 2,** Major chords are made up of a root, a major 3rd on top of that (4 half steps from the root), and a minor 3rd on top of that (3 half steps from that note). However, I am not going into this theory in this book.

Minor Chords can be created very easily from Major Chords. This will be explained in the next section. As you recall from **Lesson 6,** Minor Chords have a certain sound which makes them sound "sad".

Minor chords are made up of a root, a minor 3rd on top of that (3 half steps from the root), and a major 3rd on top of that (4 half steps from that note). However, I am not going into this theory in this book.

THE TWELVE MAJOR CHORDS

As you recall in **Lesson 2 – How to Create a Major Chord,** Major Chords (Triads) can be found by locating the 1st, 3rd, and 5th notes/degrees of each scale. However, since you may not know all of the Major Scales, and I am going to make this easy for you.

On the next page you will be shown how to locate **ALL TWELVE MAJOR CHORDS**. From these chords you will be able to form EVERY OTHER TYPE OF CHORD.

Be sure to practice these until they become easy (it won't take long at all!) and once you have these memorized, you will be able to pick up a chord charts and start playing right away.

You'll notice that as you practice these chords, your HAND SHAPE does not change (or at least it changes very little). This is a great thing to remember as you are moving from one chord to the next.

Have fun with this! Do a section a day, if you would like, or go for the gusto and try memorizing them all at once!

FINDING THE TWELVE MAJOR CHORDS

These Major Chords as written are in **ROOT POSITION**. This means they are not *inverted* and the note name of the scale from which they are named is at the bottom of the chord, or the **first** note of the chord. (In other words, the C Chord is the 1st, 3rd, and 5th notes/degrees of the C Major Scale, the F Chord is made from the 1st, 3rd and 5th notes/degrees of the F Major Scale, etc.)

MAJOR CHORDS PRACTICE #1
Root Position (NOT Inverted)

Pick out the following chords with your EACH HAND, using the 5, 3, and 1 (1, 3 and 5 in Right hand) fingers for each chord. (You'll notice that your finger shape does not have to change as you move from one chord to the next.)   I've included some "clever sayings" that might help you to remember these chords and their order a bit easier.   PRACTICE these until they become easy to move between.

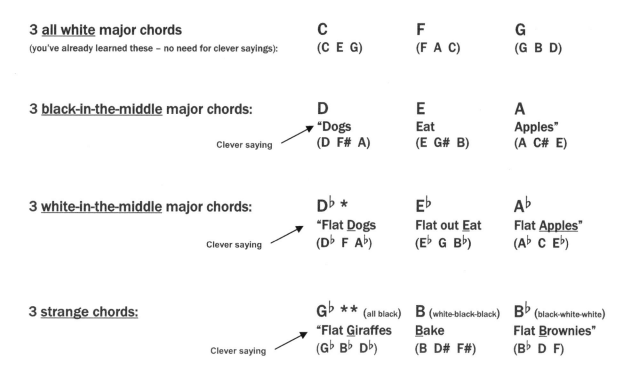

3 <u>all white</u> major chords

(you've already learned these – no need for clever sayings):

C	F	G
(C E G)	(F A C)	(G B D)

3 <u>black-in-the-middle</u> major chords:

D	E	A
"Dogs	Eat	Apples"
(D F# A)	(E G# B)	(A C# E)

Clever saying

3 <u>white-in-the-middle</u> major chords:

D♭ *	E♭	A♭
"Flat Dogs	Flat out Eat	Flat Apples"
(D♭ F A♭)	(E♭ G B♭)	(A♭ C E♭)

Clever saying

3 <u>strange chords</u>:

G♭ ** (all black)	B (white-black-black)	B♭ (black-white-white)
"Flat Giraffes	Bake	Flat Brownies"
(G♭ B♭ D♭)	(B D# F#)	(B♭ D F)

Clever saying

IMPORTANT NOTES:

The **C# chord contains the same notes as the **D♭** chord, but the note names are **C#, E#** and **G#**.*

***The **F#** chord contains the same notes as the **G♭** chord, but the note names are **F#, A#,** and **C#**.*

MAJOR CHORDS PRACTICE #2
(All Inversions)

Now practice all the Major Chords in the above order, but do so as **inversions**. Refer back to *Lesson 8 - Chord Inversions and Practice*. Do this as **block chords and also as broken chords**.

For example for the C Chord, play with **C** on the bottom, then **E** on the bottom, then **G** on the bottom, as follows:

C Root Position:	C E G
then **1st Inversion**:	E G C
then **2nd Inversion** :	G C E
then **Root Position** again:	C E G

Do this with EACH CHORD and with EACH HAND.

MINOR CHORDS

In review, a Minor Chord has the quality of sounding somewhat "sad". These are used quite often in music and many people prefer listening to music with minor chords.

FINDING THE TWELVE MINOR CHORDS

Finding a Minor Chord is quite simple. To find a **MINOR CHORD**, play the **MAJOR CHORD**, but **LOWER THE 3rd by ½ STEP**.

For example, the C Major Chord (C Chord) is made up of **C, E, and G** (the 1st, 3rd and 5th notes/degrees of the C Major Scale). To make a **C Minor Chord** out of the C Major Chord, **lower** the "**E**" (the 3rd) to an "**E♭**". So, the C Minor Chord (Cm) would be made up of **C, E♭, and G**.

The abbreviation of a MINOR CHORD is "m" "min", or "-" (example: "Dm" "Dmin",or "D-").

MINOR CHORDS PRACTICE #1
Root Position (NOT Inverted)

Practice these in the same way as the MAJOR CHORDS above, but **LOWER THE 3rd of each chord ½ step**. They will look like this:

Cm (C E♭ G)	**Fm** (F A♭ C)	**Gm** (G B♭ D)
Dm (D F A)	**Em** (E G B)	**Am** (A C E)
D♭m* (D♭ F♭ A♭)	**E♭m** (E♭ G♭ B♭)	**A♭m** (A♭ C♭ E♭)
G♭m ** (G♭ B♭♭*** D♭)	**Bm** (B D F#)	**B♭m** (B♭ D♭ F)

*The **D♭m** chord and the **C#m** chord contain the same notes but their names are **C#, E, and G#**..

The **G♭m chord and the **F#m** chord contain the same notes but their names are **F#, A and C#**.

***Note:** The B♭♭ note would be "A". This is because you "flat the flat". This is called a "double flat".

MINOR CHORDS PRACTICE #2
ALL Inversions

Now practice all the Minor Chords in the same order as you practiced the Major Chords, but do so as **inversions**. Do this as **block chords and as broken chords**.

For example for the C Chord, play with **C** on the bottom, then **E** on the bottom, then **G** on the bottom, as follows:.

C Root Position:	C E♭ G
then **1st Inversion:**	E♭ G C
then **2nd Inversion:**	G C E♭
then **Root Position** again:	C E♭ G

Do this with EACH CHORD and with EACH HAND.

KEY SIGNATURES - PART 1
What ARE They?

What is the "Key Signature"?

The **KEY SIGNATURE** is the series of sharps and flats you see located **between the clef and the Time Signature** at the beginning of each song. See examples below:

Diagram 1:   Diagram 2:

Key Signature   Key Signature

Key of G – 1 sharp – F#   **Key of F – 1 flat - Bb**
(Key of G)   **(Key of F)**

Each Major Scale has a specific **key signature,** and no two Major Scales have exactly the same key signature.   **With the exception of the Key of C, each key signature contains either one or more sharps or flats.**

WHAT DOES A KEY SIGNATURE DO?

A **Key Signature** tells you WHICH SCALE YOU WILL BE TAKING THE NOTES FROM WHEN YOU PLAY THE SONG.

When a song is written using the notes in a particular scale, this means it is written in that "Key" – in other words, **if you write a song "In the Key of C" it means that it uses the notes of the C Major Scale** (the song will have no sharps or flats because the C Major Scale has no sharps or flats).

Chord Piano Is Fun

Let me explain further:

Having created several different scales, you realize that each scale, *except for the C Major Scale*, has certain **sharps** or **flats** in it.

Take a look at **Diagram 1 on the previous page.**

As you recall, your **G Major Scale** has one sharp in it (F#). Up to this point we have just been writing the sharp **next to the F note on the scale** (see Lesson 3). However, with the use of the **Key Signature**, we can just place this sharp on the **F line** at the beginning of the song, which shows us that **every F in that song should be sharped**.

This makes it much easier than having to put sharp in front of every F in the song. This also tells us that this song is in the **KEY OF G**, because it is **using the notes in the G Major Scale** (the G Major Scale has 1 sharp).

In the same way, take a look **Diagram 2.**

This is the Key Signature for the **Key of F**. The Key Signature shows a flat on the B line of the staff because this song **uses the notes in the F Major Scale**. The Key Signature shows us that **every B that you play in that key should be flatted** because the F Major Scale has one flat.

> **REMEMBER:** With the exception of the Key of C, each key signature contains either one or more sharps or flats.

Here is what the Key of C Key Signature looks like:

Note that there is nothing in the "Key Signature" area because the Key of C (C Major Scale) has no sharps or flats.

KEY SIGNATURE IDENTIFICATION

# OF SHARPS/FLATS	KEY	VIEW OF KEY SIGNATURE	
0	C		
SHARP KEY SIGNATURES			
# OF SHARPS	KEY	VIEW OF KEY SIGNATURE	
1	G		
2	D		
3	A		
4	E		
5	B		
6	F#		
7	C#		

KEY SIGNATURE IDENTIFICATION, CONT.

FLAT KEY SIGNATURES		
NUMBER OF FLATS	**KEY**	**VIEW OF KEY SIGNATURE**
1	F	
2	B♭	
3	E♭	
4	A♭	
5	D♭	
6	G♭	
7	C♭	

EASY way to determine how many sharps or flats a key signature has:

If you add the number of sharps to the number of flats for each NOTE NAME, the answer will be "7".

For example, if you know that the key of G has 1 sharp, then the key of G$^\flat$ will have 6 flats: 1+6=7. Or, if you know that the key of B$^\flat$ has 2 flats, the key of B will have 5 sharps: 2+5=7.

QUICK REVIEW AND MEMORIZE

C (No sharps or flats):

SHARP KEY SIGNATURES

G (1 sharp)

D (2 sharps)

A (3 sharps)

E (4 sharps)

B (5 sharps)

F# (6 sharps)

C# (7 sharps)

FLAT KEY SIGNATURES

F (1 flat)

B$^\flat$ (2 flats)

E$^\flat$ (3 flats)

A$^\flat$ (4 flats)

D$^\flat$ (5 flats)

G$^\flat$ (6 flats)

C$^\flat$ (7 flats)

LESSON 10
KEY SIGNATURE PART 1
– WHAT ARE THEY?

NOTES

KEY SIGNATURES - PART 2
Order of Sharps and Flats

How do I know which notes to sharp or flat in each Key Signature?

As you saw from our last lesson, *Lesson 10,* each key signature (with the exception of the Key of C), has a collection of sharps or flats in them.

You may wonder which notes are sharped or which notes are flatted when playing a song with a particular Key Signature. For example, you may want to try to play a song with 4 sharps. However, you have not learned that scale yet and don't know which notes to sharp.

REMEMBER THIS:

**There is always an ORDER to which sharps and flats are added
to each Key Signature.**

The great thing about **Key Signatures**, is that each one builds on the other. For example, if a Key Signature has **1 sharp**, it will always be **F#**. If a Key Signature has **2 sharps**, it will always be **F#**, but then add another, which will be **C#**. If a Key Signature has **3 sharps**, it will always be **F#**, and **C#** and then add **G#**, and so on.

This also holds true for the Flat Key Signatures. The first flat will always be **B♭**, the 2nd flat will always be **E♭**, etc.

KEY SIGNATURE ORDER - SHARPS

The following is the **ORDER IN WHICH SHARPS ARE ADDED TO EACH KEY SIGNATURE** (Key Signatures based on the scales that contain SHARPS):

KEY	NUMBER OF SHARPS AND THEIR **ORDER**
G	1 SHARP – **F**
D	2 SHARPS- **F, C**
A	3 SHARPS - **F, C, G**
E	4 SHARPS - **F, C, G, D**
B	5 SHARPS - **F, C, G, D, A**
F#	6 SHARPS - **F, C, G, D, A, E**
C#	7 SHARPS - **F, C, G, D, A, E, B**

The **ORDER OF SHARPS** added to each **SHARP** Key Signature is:

F C G D A E B

An easy way to remember this would be:

Fat **C**ats **G**o **D**own **A**nd **E**at **B**reakfast
Or
Father **C**harles **G**oes **D**own **A**nd **E**nds **B**attle

You might want to try to make up your own saying to help you remember the **ORDER OF SHARPS.**

KEY SIGNATURE ORDER - FLATS

The following is the **ORDER** IN WHICH FLATS ARE ADDED TO EACH FLAT KEY
SIGNATURES (Key Signatures based on the scales that contain FLATS):

KEY	NUMBER OF FLATS AND THEIR ORDER
F	1 FLAT – **B**
B♭	2 FLATS - **B, E**
E♭	3 FLATS - **B, E, A**
A♭	4 FLATS - **B, E, A, D**
D♭	5 FLATS - **B, E, A, D, G**
G♭	6 FLATS – **B, E, A, D, G, C**
C♭	7 FLATS – **B, E, A, D, G, C, F**

This **ORDER OF FLATS** added to each **FLAT** Key Signature is:

B E A D G C F

An easy way to remember this would be:

Battle **E**nds **A**nd **D**own **G**oes **C**harles' **F**ather

You might want to try to make up your own saying to help you remember the **ORDER OF
FLATS.**

QUICK REVIEW AND MEMORIZATION

Try to memorize each Order:

ORDER OF SHARPS:

F C G D A E B

An easy way to remember this would be:

> **F**at **C**ats **G**o **D**own **A**nd **E**at **B**reakfast
> Or
> **F**ather **C**harles **G**oes **D**own **A**nd **E**nds **B**attle

ORDER OF FLATS:

B E A D G C F

An easy way to remember this would be:

> **B**attle **E**nds **A**nd **D**own **G**oes **C**harles' **F**ather

INTRODUCING 7ᵗʰ CHORDS (DOMINANT 7ᵗʰ CHORDS) (and the 4ᵗʰ MOST IMPORTANT CHORD!)

What are 7ᵗʰ Chords (Dominant 7ᵗʰ Chords)?

When you see a song that has a chord symbol that has a **"7"** after it (such as "**G⁷**"), this is called a **"Dominant 7th Chord"**. (This is not the same as the "**Gmaj7 chord**", which will be discussed in *Lesson 24 – Building Other Types of Chords*.)

Dominant 7th Chords (7ᵗʰ Chords) are used quite often in music, and are chords symbols you will see all of the time as you are reading from lead sheets (chord charts). They are used very often in jazz music.

Why are they called this?

Remember in *Lesson 6 – Scales and Their Chords*, where you learned that each degree of the scale has a **Technical Name**?

	C̲	Dm	Em	F	G	Am	Bdim	C̲
Chord Degrees →	(1- Root)	(2)	(3)	(4)	(5)	(6)	(7)	(8 – Octave (same as root)
Roman Numeral Notation →	I	ii	iii	IV	V	vi	vii°	I
Technical Name →	Tonic	Supertonic	Mediant	Sub- dominant	Dominant	Submediant	Leading Tone	Tonic

Dominant 7ths are called "**Dominant**" because they are **built from the V Chord** (using the SCALE of the V chord), which is the **DOMINANT Chord** of the Major Scale (in the above example, we are using the C Major Scale).

NOTE: 7th chords can be built from any chord in the scale, really, but are built most often from the **V** chord because of the sound that it gives in combining with the other chords of the song. Don't get too caught up on the word "**Dominant**" – I am just trying to briefly explain WHY it is called this. We are more concerned with HOW to CREATE this chord, than WHY it is called this.

How do you build a 7th Chord (Dominant 7th Chord)?

To find a **7th chord**, you are to **play the Major Chord that is named** (example: **G**), and then **ADD** the **lowered (flatted) 7th degree of THAT scale** (the G Major Scale) **to that chord**.

FIND THE G⁷ CHORD:

Remember that the **G Chord** consists of the **1st**, **3rd**, and **5th degrees** of the **G Scale (G B D)** (see **Lesson 3 – Building the G Chord**). To find the G⁷ chord, **ADD the lowered 7th note of** this scale to the **G Chord**:

Name the 1st degree of the G Scale: _____
Name the 3rd degree of the G Scale: _____
Name the 5th degree of the G Scale: _____
Name the 7th degree of the G Scale: _____   Now, lower it ½ step: _____

So, the **G⁷** chord consists of these notes: <u>G</u>   <u>B</u>   <u>D</u>   <u>F</u>
                                                    (Root) 3rd   5th   lowered (flatted) 7th

Note: The 7th note of the G scale is actually F#, but we <u>lower it (flat it) ½ step</u> and use that note – which is **F**.

EASY WAY TO FIND A 7th!

An easy way to find the **7th chord** is to play the Major Chord, then **add the note that is 1 whole step down from the octave** of the scale. For example, the octave of "G" is the next higher "G". One whole step down from "**G**" is "**F**".

THERE ARE NOW *FOUR* MOST IMPORTANT FAMILY CHORDS!

Your **7th Chord** is NOW ADDED to your list of **MOST IMPORTANT FAMILY CHORDS**.
So, in the **Key of C**, your **FOUR MOST IMPORTANT FAMILY CHORDS ARE**:

C   F   G   and   G⁷
I   IV   V   V⁷

PRACTICE #1
Chord Practice
7th Chords – Root Form (NO Inversions)
"ROOT CADENCE FORM"

Try playing the **G⁷** Chord with your left hand. Practice moving back and forth between the **C** Chord, the **F** Chord and the **G** Chord and the **G⁷** Chord in the ROOT POSITION (not inverted). Practice this until it becomes easy for you.

Example:

Play **C** Chord (**C E G**),
then
F Chord (**F A C**)
then
G Chord (**G B D**)
then
C Chord again
then
G⁷ Chord (**G B D F**)
then
C Chord again.

Do the same with your right hand.

PRACTICE #2
Song Practice
7th Chords - Root Form (NO Inversions)

Practice the next two songs, playing your chords in **ROOT POSITION** (not inversions):

C Chord (I Chord) played as **"C-E-G"**
F Chord (IV Chord) played as **"F-A-C"**
G Chord (V7) Chord) played as **"G-B-D-F"**

DOWN IN THE VALLEY

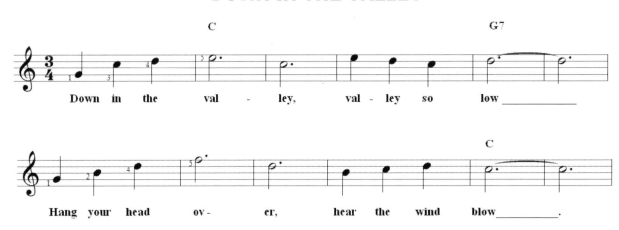

SKIP TO MY LOU

PRACTICE #3
Chord Practice
7th Chords <u>WITH</u> Inversions
"INVERSION CADENCE FORM"

You are now going to learn how to play the 7th chord as an "**inversion**" (see *Lesson 8 – Chord Inversions*).

When the 7th chord is **inverted**, it is a bit different than when the other chords are inverted. Typically, in an inverted chord, you play ALL the notes of the chord. However, with the *inverted 7th chord,* we often **DROP the 5th** of the chord to make it easier to play and **THEN** the chord is inverted.

Here is the G7 Chord in ROOT FORM:

<u>G</u>   <u>B</u>   <u>D</u>   <u>F</u>
(1st)   (3rd) (5th) (dropped) (lowered 7th)

Here is the G7 Chord in INVERTED FORM (1st inversion) with the 5th dropped:

<u>B</u>   <u>F</u>   <u>G</u>
(3rd) (lowered 7th) (1st)

Note: To play the **G7 Chord**, instead of playing **G, B, D** and **F**, you will play **G, B,** and **F** (having DROPPED the "D" out of the chord), and then you will **INVERT** it (as above):

INSTRUCTIONS:

Try playing the **G7 Chord** with your left hand **as an inversion** (see above). Practice moving back and forth between the **C Chord**, the **F Chord** and the **G Chord** and the **G7**as follows (I call this the "**Inversion Cadence Form**":

Play **C** Chord (**C E G** – Root Position)
then **F** Chord (**C F A** – 2nd Inversion)
then **C** Chord again
then **G** Chord (**B D G** –1st Inversion)
then **C** Chord again
then **G7** Chord (**B F G** – 1st Inversion with 5th dropped)
then **C** Chord again

You will practice all of your MOST IMPORTANT FAMILY CHORDS this way throughout this Lesson Book.

PRACTICE #4
Song Practice
7th chords <u>WITH</u> Inversions

Practice the next songs, playing your chords in **INVERTED POSITION** (**1st** Inversion):

C Chord (I Chord) played as **"C-E-G"**
F Chord (IV Chord) played as **"C-F-A"**
G7 Chord (V^7) Chord) played as **"B-F-G"**

THIS OLD MAN

THIS OLD MAN HE PLAYED ONE, HE PLAYED "NICK NACK" ON MY DRUM WITH A

"NICK NACK PAD-DY WACK GIVE A DOG A BONE", THIS OLD MAN CAME ROL-LING HOME.

YANKEE DOODLE

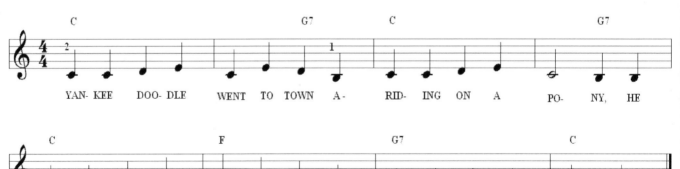

YAN-KEE DOO-DLE WENT TO TOWN A- RID-ING ON A PO- NY, HE

STUCK A FEA-THER IN HIS HAT AND CALLED IT MAC-A- RO-NI!

SILENT NIGHT

Also try the songs in Practice #2 with inversions.

NOTES

Chord Piano Is Fun!

Lesson 13

KEY OF G FAMILY CHORDS

As you recall from *Lesson 6 – Scales and Their Chords*, each key contains a set of
FAMILY CHORDS.
These are chords that belong in a certain "key" or a certain scale.

Review of notes in the G Major Scale (refer back to *Lesson 3*):

	G	A	B	C	D	E	F#	G	
Degrees of the scale →	1	2	3	4	5	6	7	8	
	I	ii	iii	IV	V	vi	vii°	VIII	← Roman Numerals

Review:

Recalling from *Lesson 6*, you will notice that some of the Roman Numerals are in **UPPER CASE** and some of them are in **LOWER CASE**. These "cases" tell us **WHAT KIND** of Chord these chords will be – either **Major, Minor,** or **Diminished**.

BECAUSE WE ARE IN THE "KEY OF G", WE NEED TO USE THE NOTES IN THE "G SCALE" TO CREATE OUR "KEY OF G FAMILY CHORDS."

Because the "G Scale" has one sharp (F#), we must use the **F#** rather than the **F** whenever we come to this note.

Because of this, not all of the triads/chords will be MAJOR CHORDS. **Some** will be **MAJOR,** but some will also be either **MINOR** or **DIMINISHED**.

FAMILY CHORDS PRACTICE

An easy way to practice these chords, is to just **play TRIADS (THREE NOTE CHORDS)** all the way up the G Scale, one after the other, with each note in the scale being the **ROOT of a TRIAD.**

You are going to use **ONLY the notes in the G Scale** to create your triads. This means, every time you come to an **F**, you must play the **F#** because the **F is <u>sharped</u> (raised ½ step) in the Key of G.**

Use the **1st finger**, **3rd finger**, and **5th finger** of each hand.

Here is how it would look on the treble staff with your right hand:

| G | Am | Bm | C | D | Em | F#dim | G |
| I | ii | iii | IV | V | vi | vii° | I |

Also play the triads with your **left** hand, beginning on **Bass G**.

All of the above TRIADS/CHORDS are considered FAMILY CHORDS in the Key of G, and will show up in many songs written in the Key of G!

THE THREE (NO, FOUR!) MOST IMPORTANT CHORDS IN THE KEY OF G

We are now going to play some songs in the **"Key of G"**. This means that we will be using the notes from the **G Scale** to play with our **right hand**, and the **MOST IMPORTANT CHORDS in the Key of G** to play with our **left hand.**

As you remember from *Lesson 13*, the G Scale has certain **FAMILY CHORDS. These chords are built from each note of the scale**. Just as with the notes of the scale, each CHORD (triad) of the scale also has a **Roman Numeral** notation. (Also refer back to *Lesson 6– SCALES AND THEIR CHORDS.*)

Review of chords in the G Major Scale (refer back to *Lesson 13*):

	G	Am	Bm	C	D	Em	F#dim	G ←	Triads built on notes of the scale.
Degrees of the scale →	1	2	3	4	5	6	7	8	
	I	ii	iii	IV	V	vi	vii	VIII ←	Roman Numeral Notation for degree of the scale and TYPE of chord

Remember, to find these **THREE MOST IMPORTANT CHORDS** for any key, we look for the **I, IV,** and **V** Chords of that scale. In addition to this, we are going to add the **V⁷ Chord**, so we now have **THE FOUR MOST IMPORTANT CHORDS.**

KEY OF G MOST IMPORTANT FAMILY CHORDS

Find the <u>named chord</u> from the ABOVE chart, and <u>then write the notes of the chord</u> on the lines provided *(if necessary, please see **Lesson 9 – The Twelve Major Chords**, to review these chords).*

I Chord =	_____	Notes in the I Chord are:	_____	_____	_____	
IV Chord =	_____	Notes in the IV Chord are:	_____	_____	_____	
V Chord =	_____	Notes in the V Chord are:	_____	_____	_____	
V⁷ Chord =	_____	Notes in the V⁷ Chord* are:	_____	_____	_____	___*

*The V⁷ chord is made by playing the named chord, and then add **the lowered 7th** degree of the scale to the V chord **OR**, if you don't know the notes to the scale, just add the note which is **one whole step lower** than the octave. (**Be sure to review *Lesson 12 – Introducing 7th Chords.***)

PRACTICE #1

1. **"ROOT CADENCE FORM"** (Refer back to *Lesson 12*):

   Practice moving back and forth between **THE FOUR MOST IMPORTANT CHORDS** in **Root Position**. Play as follows:

   > G = G B D
   > C = C E G
   > G
   > D = D F# A
   > G
   > D^7 = D F# A C
   > G

2. **"INVERSION CADENCE FORM"** (Refer back to *Lesson 12*):

   Practice moving back and forth between **THE FOUR MOST IMPORTANT CHORDS** with **Chord Inversions***. Play as follows:

   > G = G B D
   > C = G C E
   > G
   > D = F# A D
   > G
   > D^7* = F# C D*
   > G

*Remember, when playing the 7th Chord in an **inversion**, we often **DROP** the 5th of the chord and **THEN invert it** to make it easier to play (review *Lesson 12*). In this case, we would drop the "A", (which is the 5th in the D^7 chord) since the D^7 chord is actually:

> <u>D</u>   <u>F#</u>   <u>A</u>   <u>C</u>
> (**1**st)   (**3**rd)   (**5**th)   (lowered 7th)

So, inverted it would be:

> <u>F#</u>   <u>C</u>   <u>D</u>

PRACTICE #2

TRY THESE SONGS IN THE KEY OF G
G, C, D and D⁷ Chords
(I, IV, V and V⁷ Chords)

Practice the following songs in the **Key of G**. Notice that the "Key Signature" is at the beginning of the song before the Time Signature. This shows that each **F** will be sharped.

Play the **melody** with your right hand, remembering to sharp all of the F's in the song. Play the **chord** with your left hand exactly as noted.

JINGLE BELLS
Key of G - 1 sharp (F#)
G C, and D Chords (I, IV, and V Chords)

G Chord (I Chord) played as "G-B-D"
C Chord (IV Chord) played as "G-C-E"
D Chord (V Chord) played as "D-F#-A"

Chord Piano Is Fun!

TWINKLE, TWINKLE

Key of G - 1 sharp (F#)
G, C, and D Chords (I, IV, and V^7 Chords)

G Chord (I Chord) played as "G-B-D"
C Chord (IV Chord) played as "G-C-E"
D^7 Chord (V^7 Chord) played as "F#-C-D"

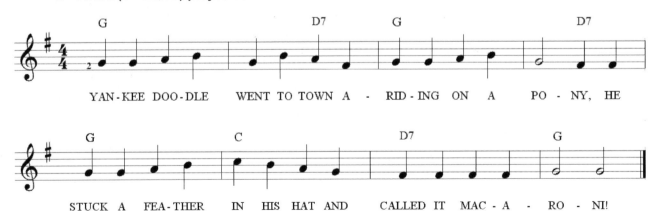

YANKEE DOODLE

Key of G – 1 sharp (F#)
G, C, and D^7 Chords (I, IV, and V^7 Chords)

G Chord (I Chord) played as "G-B-D"
C Chord (IV Chord) played as "G-C-E"
D^7 Chord (V^7 Chord) played as "F#-C-D"

Chord Piano Is Fun!

KEY OF F FAMILY CHORDS

As you recall from *Lesson 6 – Scales and Their Chords*, each key contains a set of
FAMILY CHORDS.
These are chords that belong in a certain "key" or a certain scale.

Review of notes in the F Major Scale (refer back to *Lesson 4*):

	F	G	A	B♭	C	D	E	F	
Degrees of the scale →	1	2	3	4	5	6	7	8	
	I	ii	iii	IV	V	vi	vii°	VIII	← Roman Numerals

Review:

Recalling from **Lesson 6**, you will notice that some of the Roman Numerals are in **UPPER CASE** and some of them are in **LOWER CASE**. These "cases" tell us **WHAT KIND** of Chord these chords will be – either **Major, Minor,** or **Diminished**.

BECAUSE WE ARE IN THE "KEY OF F", WE NEED TO USE THE NOTES IN THE "F SCALE" TO CREATE OUR "KEY OF F FAMILY CHORDS."

Because the "F Scale" has one flat (**B♭**), whenever the triads/chords that has a "B" in it, we create must use the **B♭** rather than the **B** whenever we come to this note.

Because of this, not all of the triads/chords will be MAJOR CHORDS. **Some** will be **MAJOR**, but some will also be either **MINOR** or **DIMINISHED**.

FAMILY CHORDS PRACTICE

An easy way to practice these chords, is to just play **TRIADS (THREE NOTE CHORDS)** all the way up the F Scale, one after the other, with each note in the scale being the **ROOT of a TRIAD.**

You are going to use **ONLY the notes in the F Scale** to create your triads. This means, every time you come to a **"B",** you must play the **"B♭"** because the **B is flatted (lowered ½ step) in the Key of F.**

Use the 1st finger, 3rd finger, and 5th finger of each hand.

Here is how it would look on the treble staff with your right hand:

F	Gm	Am	B♭	C	Dm	Edim	F
I	ii	iii	IV	V	vi	vii°	I

Also play the triads with your **left** hand, beginning on **Bass F.**

All of the above TRIADS/CHORDS are considered FAMILY CHORDS in the Key of F, and will show up in many songs written in the Key of F!

Chord Piano Is Fun!

THE THREE (NO, FOUR!) MOST IMPORTANT CHORDS IN THE KEY OF F

We are now going to play some songs in the **"Key of F"**. This means that we will be using the notes from the **F Scale** to play with our **right hand**, and the **THREE (no, FOUR!) MOST IMPORTANT CHORDS** in the Key of F to play with our **left hand**.

As you remember from *Lesson 15 – Key of F Family Chords*, the F Scale has certain **FAMILY CHORDS**. **These chords are built from each note of the scale.** Just as with the notes of the scale, each CHORD (triad) of the scale also has a **Roman Numeral** notation. (Also refer back to *Lesson 6 – Scales and Their Chords*.)

Review of chords in the F Major Scale (refer back to *Lesson 15*):

	F	Gm	Am	B♭	C	Dm	Edim	F	← Triads built on notes of the scale.
Degrees of the scale →	1	2	3	4	5	6	7	8	
	I	ii	iii	IV	V	vi	vii°	VIII	← Roman Numerals

Remember, to find these **THREE MOST IMPORTANT CHORDS** for any key, we look for the **I**, **IV**, and **V** Chords of that scale. In addition to this, we are going to add the **V⁷** Chord, so we now have **THE <u>FOUR</u> MOST IMPORTANT CHORDS.**

KEY OF F MOST IMPORTANT FAMILY CHORDS

Find the <u>named chord</u> from the ABOVE chart, and <u>then write the notes of the chord</u> on the lines provided *(if necessary, please see **Lesson 9 – The Twelve Major Chords**, to review these chords).*

I Chord = _____	Notes in the I Chord are:	___	___	___	
IV Chord = _____	Notes in the IV Chord are:	___	___	___	
V Chord = _____	Notes in the V Chord are:	___	___	___	
V⁷ Chord = _____	Notes in the V⁷ Chord* are:	___	___	___	___*

*The V⁷ chord is made by playing the named chord, and then add the **lowered 7th** degree of the scale to the **V** (5) chord **OR**, if you don't know the notes to the scale, just add the note which is 1 whole step lower than the octave. (Be sure to review *Lesson 12 – Introducing 7th Chords*.)

Chord Piano Is Fun!

PRACTICE #1

1. **"ROOT CADENCE FORM"** (Refer back to *Lesson 12)*:

   Practice moving back and forth between **THE FOUR MOST IMPORTANT CHORDS** in **Root Position.** Play as follows:

F =	F A C
B♭ =	B♭ D F
F	
C =	C E G
F	
C⁷ =	C E G B♭
F	

2. **"INVERSION CADENCE FORM"** (Refer back to *Lesson 12)*:

   Practice moving back and forth between **THE FOUR MOST IMPORTANT CHORDS** with **Chord Inversions*.** Play as follows:

F =	F A C
B♭ =	F B♭ D
F	
C =	E G C
F	
C⁷ =	E B♭ C*
F	

***Remember,** when playing the **7ᵗʰ Chord** in an **inversion**, we often **DROP** the **5ᵗʰ** of the chord and **THEN invert it to 1ˢᵗ inversion** to make it easier to play (review *Lesson 12 – Introducing 7ᵗʰ Chords).* In this case, we would drop the "G" (which is the 5ᵗʰ in the C⁷ chord), since the C⁷ chord is actually:

<u>C</u>	<u>E</u>	<u>G</u>	<u>B♭</u>
(1ˢᵗ)	(3ʳᵈ)	(5ᵗʰ)	(lowered 7ᵗʰ)

So, inverted it would be:

<u>E</u>	<u>B♭</u>	<u>C</u>

PRACTICE #2

TRY THESE SONGS IN THE KEY OF F
F, B♭, C and C⁷ Chords
(I, IV, V and V⁷ Chords)

Practice the following songs in the **Key of F**. Notice that the "Key Signature" is at the beginning of the song before the Time Signature. This shows that each **B** will be flatted.

Play the **melody** with your right hand, remembering to flat all of the B's in the song. Play the **chord** with your left hand exactly as noted.

JINGLE BELLS
Key of F – 1 flat (B♭)
F, B♭, C Chords (I, IV, and V Chords)

F Chord (IV Chord)) played as "F-A-C"
B♭ Chord (IV Chord) played as "F -B♭-D"
C Chord (IV Chord) played as "E-G-C"

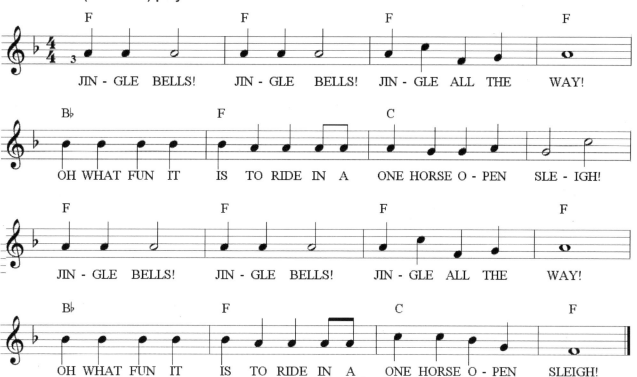

LESSON 16
THE THREE (NO, 4!) MOST IMPORTANT
CHORDS IN THE KEY OF F

TWINKLE, TWINKLE

Key of F – 1 flat (B♭)
F, B♭, C⁷ Chords (I, IV, and V⁷ Chords)

F Chord (IV Chord)) played as "F-A-C"
B♭ Chord (IV Chord) played as "F -B♭-D"
C⁷ Chord (V⁷ Chord) played as "E-B♭-C"

YANKEE DOODLE

Key of F – 1 flat (B♭)
F, B♭, C⁷ Chords (I, IV, and V⁷ Chords)

F Chord (IV Chord)) played as "F-A-C"
B♭ Chord (IV Chord) played as "F -B♭-D"
C⁷ Chord (V⁷ Chord) played as "E-B♭-C"

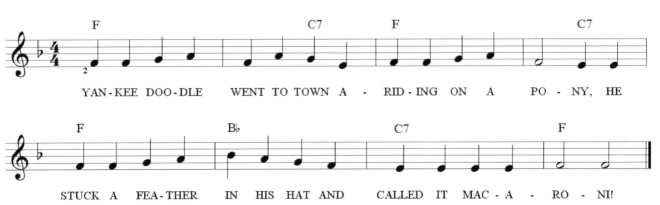

Chord Piano Is Fun!

THE TWELVE 7TH AND MINOR 7TH CHORDS

You've been briefly introduced to 7th Chords in *Lesson 12 – Introducing 7th Chords*. We are now going to practice ALL of the 7th Chords. To do this, we are going to **ADD the LOWERED 7th** to each Major Chord to create the 7th Chord (OR, add the note which is 1 whole step lower than the octave (see *Lesson 12*).

PRACTICE #1
7th Chords – Root Position (NO Inversions)

Practice these the same way you practiced the **TWELVE MAJOR AND MINOR CHORDS** (see *Lesson 9 – Twelve Major and Minor Chords*). Do this as broken chords. Do this with each hand.

3 <u>all white</u> + 7th chords:	C7 (C E G B♭)	F7 (F A C E♭)	G7 (G B D F)
3 <u>black-in-the-middle</u> + 7th chords:	D7 (D F# A C)	E7 (E G #B D)	A7 (A C# E G)
3 <u>white-in-the middle</u> + 7th chords:	D♭7* (D♭ F A♭ C♭)	E♭7 (E♭ G B♭ D♭)	A♭7 (A♭ C E♭ G♭)
3 <u>strange</u> + 7th chords	G♭7** (G♭ B♭ D♭ F♭)	B7 (B D# F# A)	B♭7 (B♭ D F A♭)

*The **D♭7** chord and the **C#7** chord contain the same notes, but their names are **C#, E#** and **G#** and **B**.
The **G♭7 chord and the **F#7** chord contain the same notes but their names are **F#, A#,** and **C#** and **E**.

Practice **EACH SECTION OF CHORDS** at a time, until you can play them smoothly. Then move to the next section.

PRACTICE #2
7th Chords – ALL Inversions

Now practice all the 7th chords in the above order, but do so as **inversions**, but **DO NOT drop the 5th** from the chord – play all the notes.

For example for the C Chord, play with **C** on the bottom, then **E** on the bottom, then **G** on the bottom, then **B**♭ on the bottom as follows:

C^7 Root Position:	C E G B♭
then **1st Inversion**:	E G B♭ C
then **2nd Inversion**:	G B♭ C E
then **3rd Inversion**:	B♭ C E G
then **C^7 Root Position** again:	C E G B♭

Do this with EACH CHORD and EACH HAND.

PRACTICE #3
7th Chords –Drop the 5th And Invert the Chord

Practice all the 7th chords but **DROP the 5th** from the chord and play it in **1st inversion** (see *Lesson 12 – Introducing 7th Chords*). Do this as **block chords and also as broken chords.** Do this with each chord and each hand.

3 <u>all white</u> + 7th chords:	C⁷ (E B♭ C)	F⁷ (A E♭ F)	G⁷ (B F G)
3 <u>black-in-the-middle</u> + 7th chords:	D⁷ (F# C D)	E⁷ (G# D E)	A⁷ (C# G A)
3 <u>white-in-the middle</u> + 7th chords:	D♭⁷* (F C♭ D♭)	E♭⁷ (G D♭ E♭)	A♭⁷ (C G♭ A♭)
3 <u>strange</u> + 7th chords:	G♭⁷** (B♭ F♭ G♭)	B⁷ (D# A B)	B♭⁷ (D A♭ B♭)

*The D♭⁷ chord and the C#⁷ chord contain the same notes, but their names different
**The G♭⁷ chord and the F#⁷ chord contain the same notes but their names are different.

PRACTICE #4
7th Chords –ALL Inversions with DROPPED 5th

Now practice all the 7th chords with the **DROPPED 5th** but do so as **INVERSIONS**. Do this as **block chords and also as broken chords.** Do this with each chord and each hand.

Example:

C^7 Root Position:	C E B$^\flat$
then **1st Inversion:**	E B$^\flat$ C
then **2nd Inversion:**	B$^\flat$ C E
then **C^7 Root Position** again:	C E B$^\flat$

MINOR 7TH CHORDS

To create **MINOR 7th CHORDS**, play the **MAJOR** Chord, but **LOWER THE 3rd ½ STEP** and **ADD A LOWERED 7th** (**OR**, add the note which is **1 whole step lower** than the octave (see **Lesson 12 – 7th Chords**).

A **Minor 7th chord** will be abbreviated with a **"m"**, **"min"**, or **"-"** and then **"7"** after the chord name. **For example: "Gm7", "Gmin7" or "G-7" means "G Minor 7th Chord".**

PRACTICE #1
Minor 7th Chords – Root Position (NOT Inverted)

Practice these in the same way as the **MINOR CHORDS** in **Lesson 9** and above. They will look like this:

Cm7
(C E♭ G B♭)

Fm7
(F A♭ C E♭)

Gm7
(G B♭ D F)

Dm7
(D F A C)

Em7
(E G B D)

Am7
(A C E G)

D♭m7*
(D♭ F♭ A♭ C♭)

E♭m7
(E♭ G♭ B♭ D♭)

A♭m7
(A♭ C♭ E♭ G♭)

G♭m7**
(G♭ B♭♭*** D♭ F♭)

Bm7
(B D F# A)

B♭m7
(B♭ D♭ F A♭)

*The **D♭m7** chord and the **C#m7** chord contain the same notes, but their names are **C#, E, G#** and **B**.

The **G♭m7 chord and the **F#m7** chord contain the same notes but their names are **F#, A, C#** and **E**.

***Note: The B♭♭ note would be "A". This is because you "flat the flat". This is called a "double flat".

LESSON 17
THE TWELVE 7TH AND MINOR 7TH CHORDS

PRACTICE #2
Minor 7th Chords – Root Position –ALL Inversions

Now practice all the Minor 7th Chords in the same order, but do so as **inversions**. Do this as **block chords and also as broken chords.** Do this with each chord and each hand.

For example for the C Chord, play with **C** on the bottom, then **E♭** on the bottom, then **G** on the bottom, then **B♭** on the bottom as follows:.

Cm⁷ Root Position:	C E♭ G B♭
then **1ˢᵗ Inversion:**	E♭ G B♭ C
then **2ⁿᵈ Inversion:**	G B♭ C E♭
then **3ʳᵈ Inversion:**	B♭ C E♭ G
then **Cm⁷ Root Position** again:	C E♭ G B♭

PRACTICE #3
Minor 7th Chords – Drop the 5th and Invert the Chord

Practice all the Minor 7th chords **DROP the 5th** from the chord and play it in **1st inversion** (see *Lesson 12 – Introducing 7th Chords*). Do this as **block chords and also as broken chords.** Do this with each chord and each hand.

Cm⁷
(E♭ B♭ C)

Fm⁷
(A♭ E♭ F)

Gm⁷
(B♭ F G)

Dm⁷
(F C D)

Em⁷
(G D E)

Am⁷
(C G A)

D♭⁷*
(F♭(E) C♭ D♭)

E♭⁷
(G♭ D♭ E♭)

A♭⁷
(C♭ (B) G♭ A♭)

G♭m⁷**
(B♭♭*** F♭ G♭)

Bm⁷
(D A B)

B♭m⁷
(D♭ A♭ B♭)

The **D♭m⁷ chord and the **C#m⁷** chord contain the same notes, but their names different*
***The **G♭m⁷** chord and the **F#m⁷** chord contain the same notes but their names are different.*

***Note: The B♭♭ note would be "A". This is because you "flat the flat". This is called a "double flat".

LESSON 17
THE TWELVE 7ᵀᴴ AND MINOR 7ᵀᴴ CHORDS

PRACTICE #4
Minor 7th Chords –ALL Inversions with DROPPED 5th

Now practice all the Minor 7th chords with the **DROPPED 5th** but do so as **INVERSIONS**. Do this as **block chords and also as broken chords.** Do this with each chord and each hand.

Example:
  Cm⁷ Root Position with dropped 5th: C E♭ B♭
  then **1st Inversion:**   E♭ B♭ C
  then **2nd Inversion:**   B♭ C E♭
  Cm⁷ Root Position with dropped 5th :   C E♭ B♭

MINOR SCALES (KEYS)
Using the "A Minor" Scale

We have been working with the **Major Scales** up to this point in our lesson book. We will now embark onto other scales, and in this case we will be working with **MINOR SCALES**.

In this lesson we will be using the **A Minor Scale** because it is the easiest to work with. Just as with the C Major Scale, songs written with the notes of the A Minor Scale are called "being in the Key of A Minor". This applies to every MINOR SCALE.

MINOR SCALES have a certain quality which makes them sound somewhat "sad". Many songs are written based on these minor scales, just as many songs are based on the notes in the major scales.

THE RELATIVE MINOR SCALE – What Is It?

Each Major Scale has a "**COUSIN**", or a "**Relative**" – called a **RELATIVE MINOR SCALE**. Think of this scale as the "Sad Cousin". The MINOR SCALE has the **SAME KEY SIGNATURE** as its MAJOR SCALE cousin.

Each Major Scale's "Sad Minor Cousin" is easy to find. He lives **a block and a half down** the street from his Major Scale cousin. In other words, if you think of each key on the piano being a "block", you would find the ROOT NOTE of the Minor Scale down a **step and a half** from the ROOT NOTE of any Major Scale.

For example: We know that the C Scale begins on "C". To find its Relative Minor, go **DOWN one and a half steps** to find the ROOT NOTE of its sad cousin, the **Relative Minor**. So, if you go down 1½ steps from C, you get to "A". So, the **A MINOR SCALE** is the Relative Minor Scale to the **C MAJOR SCALE**. It starts on A and ends on A.

The Relative Minor Scale can have other names, based upon the types of adjustments made to the scale.

THREE TYPES OF MINOR SCALES

NATURAL MINOR SCALE

The **Natural Minor Scale** is what we call **the Relative Minor Scale that has NO adjustments** made to it.

Here is a diagram of the A Natural Minor Scale (also just known as the "A Minor Scale"):

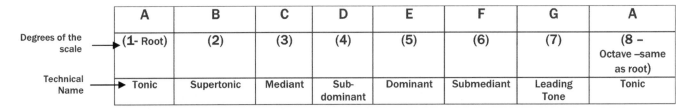

	A	B	C	D	E	F	G	A
Degrees of the scale →	(1- Root)	(2)	(3)	(4)	(5)	(6)	(7)	(8 – Octave –same as root)
Technical Name →	Tonic	Supertonic	Mediant	Sub-dominant	Dominant	Submediant	Leading Tone	Tonic

Here is how the **A Relative (Natural) Minor Scale** (also just known as the **A Minor Scale**) would look on the staff, both going up and going down (ascending and descending):

A B C D   E F G A   A G F E   D C B A

There are two other Minor Scales, and these notes DO have adjustments made to the notes in the scale. These are the **HARMONIC MINOR SCALE** and the **MELODIC MINOR SCALE.**

HARMONIC MINOR SCALES

In the **HARMONIC MINOR SCALE**, the **7th** note of the Relative (Natural) Minor Scale is RAISED (sharped) ½ STEP both ascending (going up) and descending (going down) the scale.

Here is how the **A Harmonic Minor Scale** would look on the staff, both ascending (going up) and descending (going down):

A B C D   E F G# A   A G# F E   D C B A

MELODIC MINOR SCALES

In the **MELODIC MINOR SCALE, both** the **6th** and **7th** notes of Relative (Natural) Minor Scale are RAISED (sharped) ½ STEP as you ascend (go up) the scale, but while descending (going down) the scale you return to the Natural Minor (Relative Minor) Scale.

Here is how the **A Harmonic Minor Scale** would look on the staff, both ascending and descending:

A B C D   E F# G# A   A G F E   D C B A

Remember: Songs that are written with the notes in a certain scale are called being in that **"Key"**. In the case of **Minor Scales**, you would not call a key a **HARMONIC MINOR KEY** or a **MELODIC MINOR KEY.** You would just say that something is written in the **"Key of A Minor"**, or whichever minor key you are in.

LESSON 18
MINOR SCALES

MINOR SCALES PRACTICE

Practice these Minor Scales along with the Major Scales until you are comfortable with them. Refer to **Addendum 1 - *Major and Minor Scales*** for fingering.

1.   First play the **Major Scale**

      THEN, play its RELATIVE MINOR by playing:

2.   The **Natural Minor Scale**

3.   then the **Harmonic Minor Scale**

4.   then the **Melodic Minor Scale**.

Chord Piano Is Fun!

MINOR KEY FAMILY CHORDS
(Using the Key of A Minor – Relative to C Major)

As you recall: FAMILY CHORDS are chords that belong in a certain "key"
or a certain scale.

In Minor Keys, there are also **THREE (no, four!) MOST IMPORTANT CHORDS**.
These chords are also the **1 Chord**, **4 Chord** and **5 Chord**; **however**, there is a slight
difference, which I will discuss shortly.

We are going to use the **A Minor Scale** because it is the easiest Minor Scale to use. The **A
Minor Scale** is the **RELATIVE MINOR** scale to the **C MAJOR SCALE**, and uses the **SAME KEY
SIGNATURE** as the **C MAJOR SCALE** (no sharps or flats) (**See Lesson 18 – Minor Scales**).

Instructions:

1. To review, play the Family Chords in the **C Major Scale**, starting on C *(refer back to*
   Lesson 6 – Scales and Their Chords *if necessary).*

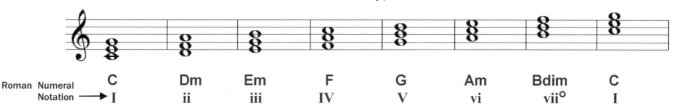

	Roman Numeral Notation →	C	Dm	Em	F	G	Am	Bdim	C
		I	ii	iii	IV	V	vi	vii°	I

2. Now, play these same chords, starting on **A**:

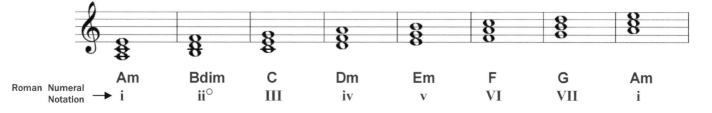

	Roman Numeral Notation →	Am	Bdim	C	Dm	Em	F	G	Am
		i	ii°	III	iv	v	VI	VII	i

NOTE: You will notice that the **Roman Numeral Notations** of the above **A Minor Scale** have
changed. For example, the **i (1) chord** is a **MINOR CHORD**, which is why the **Roman
Numeral** is in **lower case**.

3. Now, play them again, but when you get to **the 5th CHORD**, **change it to the E MAJOR CHORD** rather than the **E MINOR CHORD**.

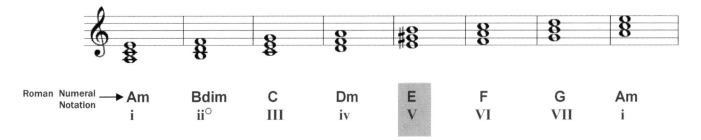

Roman Numeral Notation →	Am	Bdim	C	Dm	E	F	G	Am
	i	ii°	III	iv	V	VI	VII	i

TRIADS/CHORDS IN THE KEY OF A MINOR AND THEIR NAMES

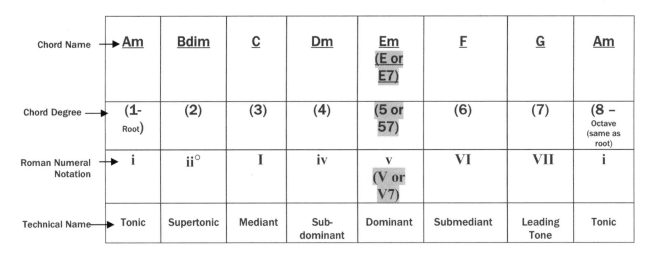

Chord Name →	**Am**	**Bdim**	**C**	**Dm**	**Em (E or E7)**	**F**	**G**	**Am**
Chord Degree →	**(1- Root)**	**(2)**	**(3)**	**(4)**	**(5 or 57)**	**(6)**	**(7)**	**(8 – Octave (same as root)**
Roman Numeral Notation →	i	ii°	I	iv	v (V or V7)	VI	VII	i
Technical Name →	Tonic	Supertonic	Mediant	Sub-dominant	Dominant	Submediant	Leading Tone	Tonic

NOTE: The **V** (5) Chord in a Minor Key is typically changed from a **MINOR CHORD** to a **MAJOR** OR **7th CHORD** because these Minor Chords are based upon the **HARMONIC MINOR SCALE**, rather than the **NATURAL MINOR SCALE** (see *Lesson 18* for review if necessary).

FINDING THE THREE (NO, FOUR!)
MOST IMPORTANT MINOR CHORDS

You will notice the **1(i)** chord is **Am**, the **4 (iv)** chord is **Dm**, and the **5 (v)** chord is **Em**. **However, we typically change the 5 Chord to the MAJOR** Chord (or the 7th Chord).

So for the Key of **A Minor**, the **THREE (no, four!) MOST IMPORTANT CHORDS** ARE:

	Am	Dm	E (or E7)
Chord Degree →	1	4	5 (or 57)
Roman Numeral → (indicates TYPE of chord)	i	iv	V* (or V7*)

*Notice that we've changed the Roman numeral of the **5 chord** to **UPPER CASE**, meaning it should be a **MAJOR** chord).

CHORD AND INVERSION PRACTICE

1. Practice moving back and forth between the Am, Dm, E, and E7 chord in **ROOT** form **(ROOT CADENCE FORM)**. (Refer back to *Lessons 8* and *12* for review of **Inversions** and **7th Chords**.)

    Play as follows:

    Am = A C E
    Dm = D F A
    Am
    E = E G# B
    Am
    E7 = E G# B D
    Am

2. Now practice moving back and forth between the **Am. Dm, E**, and **E7** chord using **INVERSIONS (INVERSION CADENCE FORM).** As you recall in *Lesson 12*, you **DROP THE 5th** of the chord when playing a 7th. Play as follows:

    Am = A C E
    Dm = A D F
    Am
    E = G# B E
    Am
    E7 = G# D E (drop the 5th, which is "B")
    Am

SONG PRACTICE

Let's try these songs in the Key of **A Minor**. Notice it uses the **same KEY SIGNATURE** as the Key of C, it's **RELATIVE MAJOR** key (no sharps or flats).   Play the melody with your right hand, and the chords with your left.. Play the chords with your left hand exactly as noted.

VOLGA BOAT SONG
Key of A Minor – No sharps or flats
Am, Dm, & E Chords (i, iv, V Chords)

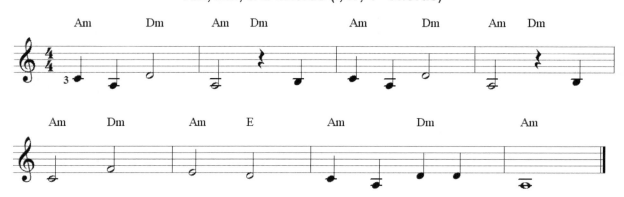

LET MY PEOPLE GO
Key of A Minor – No sharps or flats
Am, Dm, E & E7 Chords (i, iv, V & V7 Chords)

SCALES, FAMILY CHORDS, AND MOST IMPORTANT CHORDS IN THE KEY OF E MINOR
(Relative to G Major)

Review:

Referring back to **Lesson 18 – Minor Scales** and **Lesson 19 – Minor Key Family Chords,** we discovered that each **Major Key (Scale)** has a **Relative Minor Key.** To find a Major Key's Relative Minor Key, we go down **1 ½ steps** from the root note of the Major Scale. The Relative Minor Key uses the same **Key Signature** as its Relative Major Key.

FINDING THE RELATIVE MINOR KEY TO G MAJOR (E MINOR)

If you go down **1 ½** steps from the "G" in the G MAJOR SCALE, you will discover that the RELATIVE MINOR SCALE (KEY) is **E MINOR**. E Minor contains 1 sharp, just as G Major contains 1 sharp.

E NATURAL MINOR SCALE (Relative to G Major Scale):

Here are the notes in the **E Natural Minor Scale**, both ascending and descending. It contains the same exact notes as the G Major Scale, but just in a different order and starts on "E". You will be using the same fingering as you used with the G Major Scale:

E   F#   G   A   B   C   D   E   E   D   C   B   A   G   F#   G

E HARMONIC MINOR SCALE:

Remember: In the **HARMONIC MINOR SCALE**, the **7th** note of the Relative (Natural) Minor Scale is RAISED (sharped) ½ STEP both ascending (going up) and descending (going up) the scale.

Here are the notes in the **E Harmonic Minor Scale**, both ascending and descending:

E   F#   G   A   B   C   D#   E   E   D#   C   B   A   G   F#   G

E MELODIC MINOR SCALE:

Remember: In the **MELODIC MINOR SCALE**, both the **6th** and **7th** notes of Relative (Natural) Minor Scale are RAISED (sharped) ½ STEP as you ascend the scale, but while descending the scale you return to the Natural Minor (Relative Minor) Scale.

Here are the notes in the **E Melodic Minor Scale**, both ascending and descending:

E   F#   G   A   B   C#   D#   E   E   D   C   B   A   G   F#   G

PRACTICE

Practice the **G Major Scale** and then the **E Minor Scale**. (You may want to refer to **Addendum 1 - Scale Sheets Addendum** for fingering for these scales.) First play the **Major Scale**, then **its Relative Minor** by playing first the **Natural Minor Scale**, then the **Harmonic Minor Scale**, then the **Melodic Minor Scale**.

Remember: THE KEY OF E MINOR HAS **1 SHARP**, SO BE SURE TO SHARP EACH "F" AS YOU COME TO IT!

KEY OF E MINOR FAMILY CHORDS

As you learned in *Lesson 19,* each Minor Key also has its own Family Chords.

How Do I Find the E Minor Family Chords?

1. Play the Family Chords in the **G Major Scale (the E Minor Relative Major Scale)**, starting on **G (REMEMBER TO SHARP THE F'S AS THE KEY OF G MAJOR HAS ONE SHARP!):**

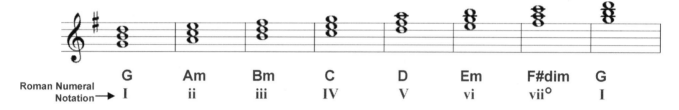

G	Am	Bm	C	D	Em	F#dim	G

Roman Numeral Notation → I · ii · iii · IV · V · vi · vii° · I

2. Now, play these same chords, starting on **E (REMEMBER TO SHARP THE F'S AS THE KEY OF E MINOR HAS ONE SHARP!):**

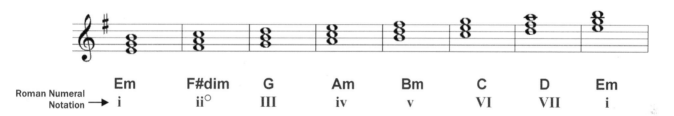

Em	F#dim	G	Am	Bm	C	D	Em

Roman Numeral Notation → i · ii° · III · iv · v · VI · VII · i

3. Now, play them again, but when you get to the FIFTH CHORD, change it to the **B MAJOR** CHORD rather than the **B MINOR** CHORD.

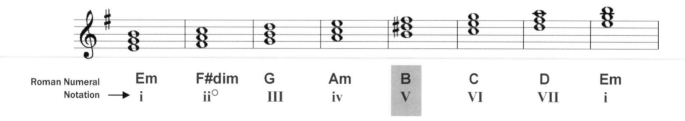

Em	F#dim	G	Am	B	C	D	Em

Roman Numeral Notation → i · ii° · III · iv · V · VI · VII · i

TRIADS/CHORDS IN THE KEY OF E MINOR AND THEIR NAMES

Chord Name →	Em	F#dim	G	Am	Bm (B or B7)	C	D	Em
Chord Degree →	(1- Root)	(2)	(3)	(4)	(5 or 57)	(6)	(7)	(8 – Octave - same as root)
Roman Numeral →	i	ii°	III	iv	v (V or V7)	VI	VII	I
Technical Name →	Tonic	Supertonic	Mediant	Sub-dominant	Dominant	Submediant	Leading Tone	Tonic

NOTE: The **V** (5) Chord in a Minor Key is typically changed from a **MINOR CHORD** to a **MAJOR** OR **7th CHORD** because these Minor Chords are based upon the **HARMONIC MINOR SCALE**, rather than the **NATURAL MINOR SCALE** (see *Lesson 18* for review if necessary).

THE THREE (NO, FOUR!) MOST IMPORTANT CHORDS IN THE KEY OF E MINOR

You will notice the **1 (i) Chord** is **Em**, the **4 (iv) Chord** is **Am**, and the **5 (v) Chord** is **Bm**. However, as you recall from *Lesson 19*, we typically change the 5 Chord to the **MAJOR** Chord (or the **7th Chord**).

So for the Key of **E Minor**, the **THREE (no, four!) MOST IMPORTANT CHORDS** ARE:

	Em	Am	B (or B7)
Chord Degree ➞	1	4	5 (or 57)
Roman Numeral ➞ (indicates TYPE of chord)	i	iv	V* (or V7*)

*Notice that we've changed the Roman numeral of the **5 chord** to **UPPER CASE**, meaning it should be a **MAJOR** chord.

CHORD AND INVERSION PRACTICE

1. Practice moving back and forth between the **Em**, **Am**, **B**, and **B⁷** chord in ROOT form, playing as follows:

    Em = E G B
    Am = A C E
    Em
    B = B D# F#
    Em
    B7 = B D# F# A
    Em

2. Now practice moving back and forth between the **Em**, **Am**, **B** and **B⁷** chord using **INVERSIONS**. As you recall in *Lesson 12*, you **DROP THE 5th** of the chord when playing a 7th. Play as follows:

    Em = E G B
    Am = E A C
    Em
    B = D# F# B (drop the 5th, which is F#)
    Em
    B7 = D# A B
    Em

SONG PRACTICE

Let's try these songs in the key of **E Minor**. Notice it uses the **same KEY SIGNATURE** as the Key of G, it's **RELATIVE MAJOR** key (1 sharp). Play the **melody** with your **right hand**, and the **chords** with your **left**. (Remember to sharp the F's in the melody, as the Key of E Minor has one sharp.) Play the chords with your left hand exactly as noted.

VOLGA BOAT SONG
Key of E Minor – 1 sharp – F#
Em, Am, & B Chords (i, iv, V Chords)

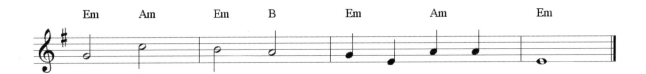

LET MY PEOPLE GO
Key of E Minor – 1 sharp – F#
Em, Am, B, & B⁷ Chords (i, iv, V, & V7 Chords)

SCALES, FAMILY CHORDS, AND MOST IMPORTANT CHORDS IN THE KEY OF D MINOR
(Relative to F Major)

Review:

Referring back to *Lesson 18 – Minor Scales* and *Lesson 19 – Minor Key Family Chords,* we discovered that each **Major Key (Scale)** has a **Relative Minor Key**. To find a Major Key's Relative Minor Key, we go down **1 ½ steps** from the root note of the Major Scale. The Relative Minor Key uses the same **Key Signature** as its Relative Major Key.

FINDING THE RELATIVE MINOR KEY TO F MAJOR
(D MINOR)

If you go down **1 ½** steps from the "F" in the F MAJOR SCALE, you will discover that the RELATIVE MINOR SCALE (KEY) is **D MINOR**. D Minor contains **1 flat**, just as F Major contains 1 flat. You will be using the same fingering as you used with the C Major Scale:

D NATURAL MINOR SCALE (RELATIVE TO F MAJOR):

Here are the notes in the D Natural Minor Scale, both ascending (going up) and descending (going down). It contains the same exact notes as the F Major Scale, but just in a different order and starts on "D".

D HARMONIC MINOR SCALE:

Remember: In the **HARMONIC MINOR SCALE**, the **7th** note of the Relative (Natural) Minor Scale is RAISED (sharped) ½ STEP both ascending (going up) and descending (going down) the scale.

Here are the notes in the D Harmonic Minor Scale, both ascending and descending:

D E F G A B♭ C# D D C# B♭ A G F E D

D MELODIC MINOR SCALE:

Remember: In the **MELODIC MINOR SCALE**, both the **6th** and **7th** notes of Relative (Natural) Minor Scale are RAISED (sharped) ½ STEP as you ascend (go up) the scale, but while descending (going down) the scale you return to the Natural Minor (Relative Minor) Scale.

Here are the notes in the D Melodic Minor Scale, both ascending and descending:

D E F G A B C# D D C B♭ A G F E D

PRACTICE

Practice the **F Major Scale** and then the **D Minor Scale**. (You may want to refer to **Addendum 1 - Scale Sheets Addendum** for **fingering** for these scales). First play the **Major Scale**, then **its Relative Minor** by playing first the Natural **Minor Scale**, then the **Harmonic Minor Scale**, then the **Melodic Minor Scale**.

Remember: THE KEY OF D MINOR HAS **1 FLAT**, SO BE SURE TO FLAT EACH "B" AS YOU COME TO IT.

KEY OF D MINOR FAMILY CHORDS

As you learned in *Lesson 19*, each Minor Key also has its own Family Chords.

How Do I Find the D Minor Family Chords?

1. Play the Family Chords in the F Major Scale, starting **on F (REMEMBER TO FLAT THE B'S AS THE KEY OF F MAJOR HAS ONE FLAT!):**

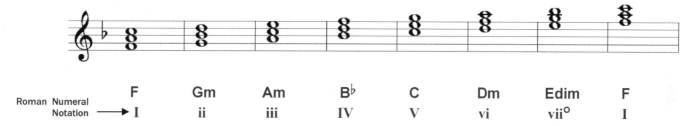

	F	Gm	Am	B♭	C	Dm	Edim	F
Roman Numeral Notation →	I	ii	iii	IV	V	vi	vii°	I

2. Now, play these same chords, starting on **D (REMEMBER TO FLAT THE B'S AS THE KEY OF D MINOR HAS ONE FLAT!):**

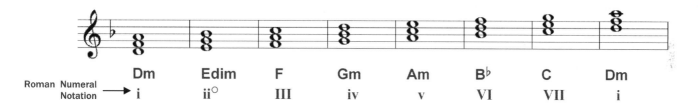

	Dm	Edim	F	Gm	Am	B♭	C	Dm
Roman Numeral Notation →	i	ii°	III	iv	v	VI	VII	i

3. Now, play them again, but when you get to the FIFTH CHORD, change it to the **A MAJOR** CHORD rather than the **A MINOR** CHORD.

	Dm	Edim	F	Gm	A	B♭	C	Dm
Roman Numeral Notation →	i	ii°	III	iv	V	VI	VII	i

THE TRIADS/CHORDS IN THE KEY OF D MINOR AND THEIR NAMES:

	Dm	Edim	F	Gm	Am (A or A7)	Bb	D	Dm
Chord Degree	(1-Root)	(2)	(3)	(4)	(5 or 57)	(6)	(7)	(8 – Octave - same as root)
Roman Numeral	i	ii°	III	iv	v (V or V7)	VI	VII	I
Technical Name	Tonic	Supertonic	Mediant	Sub-dominant	Dominant	Submediant	Leading Tone	Tonic

NOTE: The **V** (5) Chord in a Minor Key is typically changed from a **MINOR CHORD** to a **MAJOR** OR **7th CHORD** because these Minor Chords are based upon the **HARMONIC MINOR SCALE**, rather than the **NATURAL MINOR SCALE** (see *Lesson 18* for review if necessary).

THE THREE (NO, FOUR!) MOST IMPORTANT CHORDS IN THE KEY OF D MINOR

You will notice the **1 (i) Chord** is **Dm**, the **4 (iv) Chord** is **Gm**, and the **5 (v) Chord** is **Am**. However, as you recall from **Lesson 19**, we typically change the **5 Chord** to the **MAJOR** Chord (or the **7th Chord**).

So for the Key of **D Minor**, the **THREE (no, four!) MOST IMPORTANT CHORDS** ARE:

	Dm	Gm	A (or A7)
Chord Degree ➡	1	4	5 (or 57)
Roman Numeral ➡ (indicates TYPE of chord)	i	iv	V* (or V7*)

*Notice that we've changed the Roman numeral of the **5 chord** to **UPPER CASE**, meaning it should be a **MAJOR** chord.

CHORD AND INVERSION PRACTICE

1. Practice moving back and forth between the **Dm**, **Gm**, **A**, and **A7** chord in **ROOT** form, playing as follows:

   Dm = D F A
   Gm = G B♭ D
   Dm
   A = A C# E
   Dm
   A7 = A C# E G
   Dm

2. Now practice moving back and forth between the **Dm**, **Gm**, **A**, and **A7** chord using **INVERSIONS**. As you recall in **Lesson 12**, you **DROP THE 5th** of the chord when playing a 7th. Play as follows:

   Dm = D F A
   Gm = D G B♭
   Dm
   A   = C# E A (drop the 5th, which is "E")
   Dm
   A7 = C# G A
   Dm

LESSON 21
SCALES, FAMILY CHORDS, AND
MOST IMPORTANT CHORDS
- KEY OF D MINOR

SONG PRACTICE

Let's try these songs in the key of **D Minor**. Notice it uses the **same KEY SIGNATURE** as the Key of F, it's **RELATIVE MAJOR** key (1 flat). Play the **melody** with your **right hand**, and the **chords** with your **left**. (Remember to flat the B's in the melody, as the Key of D Minor has one flat.) Play the chords with your left hand exactly as noted.

VOLGA BOAT SONG
Key of D Minor – 1 flat - B♭
Dm, Gm, & A Chords (i, iv, V Chords)

LET MY PEOPLE GO
Key of D Minor – 1 flat - B♭
Dm, Gm, A, & A⁷ Chords (i, iv, V, & V⁷ Chords)

THE THREE (NO, FOUR!) MOST IMPORTANT CHORDS IN ALL *MAJOR* KEYS (FAMILY CHORDS)

Review:

Since we now know how to make scales, and chords, you need to know the **THREE (no, FOUR!) MOST IMPORTANT CHORDS** in all of the Major Keys.

These chords are the **I (1) chord, the IV (4) chord**, and the **V (5) chord**.

In addition to this, the V^7 (5^7) Chord is almost as important.

We found how to create **7th chords** in *Lesson 12 – Introducing 7th Chords.* This is where we add the **lowered 7th** degree of the scale to the **V (5)** chord. (Be sure to review *Lesson 12*.)

As you know from your scales, each note of the scale as a certain number, or "degree". Here is a review of the C Scale:

Here is a review of the C Major Scale Family Chords:

	C	Dm	Em	F	G	Am	Bdim	C	← Triad built on notes of the scale (Chord Name)
Roman Numeral → Notation	I	ii	iii	IV	V	vi	vii°	I	
	1	2	3	4	5	6	7	8	← Chord Degrees

THREE (NO, FOUR!) MOST IMPORTANT CHORDS
ALL _MAJOR_ KEYS WORKSHEET

Pull out **Addendum 1 – Major and Minor Scales**. From these sheets, find the **I (1)**, **IV (4)**, and **V (5) chords** and V^7 **(5^7) chord** of **all** the Major Scales: (Add the **lowered 7th** note in this key to the V chord to create the V^7 chord). Refer to **Addendum 2 – Most Important Chords Reference Sheet** to check answers.

Key of C:

        _____   _____   _____   _____

        I   IV   V V^7

        (1)   (4)   (5)   (5^7)

Sharp Keys

Key of G:

        I   IV   V V^7

        (1)   (4)   (5)   (5^7)

Key of D:

        I   IV   V V^7

        (1)   (4)   (5)   (5^7)

Key of A:

        I   IV   V V^7

        (1)   (4)   (5)   (5^7)

Key of E:

        I   IV   V V^7

        (1)   (4)   (5)   (5^7)

Key of B:

        I   IV   V V^7

        (1)   (4)   (5)   (5^7)

Key of F#:

        I   IV   V V^7

        (1)   (4)   (5)   (5^7)

Key of C#:

        I   IV   V V^7

        (1)   (4)   (5)   (5^7)

Flat Keys

Key of F:

I	IV	V	V^7
(1)	(4)	(5)	(5^7)

Key of B♭:

I	IV	V	V^7
(1)	(4)	(5)	(5^7)

Key of E♭:

I	IV	V	V^7
(1)	(4)	(5)	(5^7)

Key of A♭:

I	IV	V	V^7
(1)	(4)	(5)	(5^7)

Key of D♭:

I	IV	V	V^7
(1)	(4)	(5)	(5^7)

Key of G♭:

I	IV	V	V^7
(1)	(4)	(5)	(5^7)

Key of C♭:

I	IV	V	V^7
(1)	(4)	(5)	(5^7)

NOTES

THE THREE (NO, FOUR!) MOST IMPORTANT CHORDS IN ALL *MINOR* KEYS (FAMILY CHORDS)

Review:

Since we now know how to make scales, and chords, you need to know the **THREE (no, FOUR!) MOST IMPORTANT CHORDS** in all of the **MINOR** Keys.

> These chords are the **i (1) chord**, the **iv (4) chord**, and the **V (5) chord.***
>
> In addition to this, the V^7 (5^7) Chord is almost as important.
>
> We found how to create **7th chords** in *Lesson 12 – Introducing 7th Chords*. This is where we add the **lowered 7th** degree of the scale to the **V (5)** chord.

Here is a review of the A Minor Scale Family Chords (see *Lesson 19*):

Roman Numeral Notation →	Am	Bdim	C	Dm	Em	F	G	Am	← Triad built on notes of the scale (Chord Name)
	i	ii°	III	iv	v	VI	VII	I	← Chord Degrees
	1	2	3	4	5	6	7	8	

*REMINDER:

As you recall from *Lesson 19 – Minor Key Family Chords,* when we build the **MOST IMPORTANT CHORDS** of a **MINOR SCALE**, and when we play the **5 (V) chord**, we use the **MAJOR CHORD**, rather than the **MINOR CHORD**. So, the **Key of A Minor**, we would use the **E Chord** rather than the **E Minor Chord** as our **5 (V) Chord**.

THREE (NO, FOUR!) MOST IMPORTANT CHORDS – ALL *MINOR* KEYS WORKSHEET

Pull out **Addendum 1 – Major and Minor Scales**. From these sheets, find the **i (1)**, **iv (4)**, and **V (5) chords** and **V^7 (5^7) chord** of **all** the **Minor** Scales: (Add the **lowered 7th** note in this key to the V chord to create the V^7 chord).

Remember: In a Minor Key, the most common way to play the **V (5)** or **V^7 (5^7)** chord is to play a Major chord rather than a Minor chord (see **Lesson 19**).

Key of A Minor:

i	iv	V	V^7
(1)	(4)	(5)	(5^7)

Sharp Keys:

Key of E Minor:

i	iv	V	V^7
(1)	(4)	(5)	(5^7)

Key of B Minor:

i	iv	V	V^7
(1)	(4)	(5)	(5^7)

Key of F# Minor:

i	iv	V	V^7
(1)	(4)	(5)	(5^7)

Key of C# Minor:

i	iv	V	V^7
(1)	(4)	(5)	(5^7)

Key of G# Minor:

i	iv	V	V^7
(1)	(4)	(5)	(5^7)

Key of D# Minor:

i	iv	V	V^7
(1)	(4)	(5)	(5^7)

Key of A# Minor:

i	iv	V	V^7
(1)	(4)	(5)	(5^7)

FLAT KEYS

Key of D Minor:

i	iv	V	V^7
(1)	(4)	(5)	(5^7)

Key of G Minor:

i	iv	V	V^7
(1)	(4)	(5)	(5^7)

Key of C Minor:

i	iv	V	V^7
(1)	(4)	(5)	(5^7)

Key of F Minor:

i	iv	V	V^7
(1)	(4)	(5)	(5^7)

Key of B$^\flat$ Minor:

i	iv	V	V^7
(1)	(4)	(5)	(5^7)

Key of E$^\flat$ Minor:

i	iv	V	V^7
(1)	(4)	(5)	(5^7)

Key of A$^\flat$ Minor:

i	iv	V	V^7
(1)	(4)	(5)	(5^7)

Refer to **Addendum 2 – Most Important Chords Reference Sheet** to check answers and for a great way to practice them!

NOTES

BUILDING OTHER TYPES OF CHORDS

You are well on your way to being able to read ANY chord chart!

We have already learned how to create **Major, Minor, 7th**, and **Minor 7th** Chords. There are other chords that you will need to know as you play from popular song sheets and lead sheets.

In this lesson, you will learn how to create MOST types of chords that you will see on a "chord chart" – either in a Fake Book, on a song with guitar chords, or music that just shows the Chord Symbol and nothing else.

Each of these formulas refer to the "degrees of the scale". It will use a "mathematic formula" on how to create each chord. For example: to create the Diminished Chord, you will see the formula of **1+$\flat$3+$\flat$5**. This means that you take the **first note** of the scale, add the **flatted 3rd** note of the scale, and then the **flatted 5th** of the scale to create this chord. All examples are given with the C Major Chord being its example.

After reviewing these chords and their formulas, please refer to **Addendum 3 – All Types of Chords Reference Sheet** for quick reference.

MAJOR 7th CHORDS
FORMULA = 1+3+5+7

Major 7th Chords can be written with "**maj7**", "**M7**" or "$\triangle$**7** " following the name of the chord. For example: **Cmaj7, CM7,** or **C $\triangle$7**.

TO FIND THE FORMULA:

Play the **Major Chord** and **add the 7th note of the scale to the chord (NOT lowered).** This can be **SPELLED OUT** as **1+3+5+7** (notes/degrees of the scale).

Example: The **Cmaj7** chord would be:	C	E	G	B
	1	3	5	7

Note: An easy way to find a MAJOR 7th is to play the Root chord, then find the octave but go down ½ step to find the Major 7th.

DIMINISHED CHORDS
FORMULA = 1+$\flat$3+$\flat$5

Diminished Chords can by written with **"dim"** or **"°"** following the name of the chord. For example: **Cdim** or **C°**.

TO FIND THE FORMULA:

Play the **Major Chord**, but **lower** the **3rd** and the **5th** by **½ step**.

Example: The **Cdim** chord would be:	C	E$\flat$	G$\flat$
	1	$\flat$3	$\flat$5

DIMINISHED 7th CHORDS
FORMULA = 1+$\flat$3+ $\flat$5+ $\flat\flat$7

Diminished Chords can by written with **"dim7"** or **"°7"** following the name of the chord. For example: **Cdim7** or **C°7**.

The **Diminished 7th Chord** is unique, because instead of adding just a **lowered 7th** to the chord, you need to add a **"diminished 7th"** to the chord, which is **½ step lower than a lowered 7th**.

TO FIND THE FORMULA:

Play the **Diminished Chord**, and **add** a **diminished 7th** to the chord (a 7th lowered **by two ½ steps**). **Note**: This note could also be considered a "6th".

Example: The **Cdim7** chord would be:	C	E$\flat$	G$\flat$	B$^{\flat\flat}$(A)
	1	$\flat$3	$\flat$5	$\flat\flat$7

AUGMENTED CHORDS
FORMULA = 1+3+$^\sharp$5

Augmented Chords can by written with **"aug"** or **"+"** following the name of the chord. For example: **Caug** or **C+**.

TO FIND THE FORMULA:

Play the **Major Chord**, but **raise** the 5th by ½ step.

Example: The **Caug** chord would be:	C	E	G#
	1	3	#5

AUGMENTED 7TH CHORDS
FORMULA = 1+3+$^\sharp$5+$^\flat$7

Augmented Chords can by written with **"aug7"**, **"maj7#5"** or **"M7#5"** following the name of the chord. For example: **Caug7, Cmaj7#5** or **CM7#5**. The Augmented 7th Chord adds the **lowered 7th** of the scale to the Augmented Chord.

TO FIND THE FORMULA:

Play the **Augmented Chord (1st, 3rd** and **raised 5th)** and **add the lowered 7th** note of the scale.

Example: The **Caug7** chord would be:	C	F	G#	B$^\flat$
	1	4	5#	$^\flat$7

AUGMENTED MAJOR 7th CHORDS
FORMULA = 1+3+$^\sharp$5+7

Augmented Major 7th Chords can by written with **"aug7+"**, **"maj7+"**, **"M7#5**, or **"M7+"** following the name of the chord. For example: **Caug7+, Cmaj7+, CM7#5** or **CM7+**.

TO FIND THE FORMULA:

Play the **Augmented Chord (1st, 3rd and raised 5th)**, and **add** the 7th note of the scale (not lowered) to the chord.

Example: The **Caug7+** chord would be:	C	E	G#	B
	1	3	#5	7

6th CHORDS
FORMULA = 1+3+ 5+6

6th Chords can by written with "**6**" following the name of the chord. For example: **C6.**

TO FIND THE FORMULA:

Play the **Major Chord**, and **add** the **6th** note of the scale to the chord.

Example: The **C6** chord would be:	C	E	G	A
	1	3	5	6

MINOR 6th CHORDS
FORMULA = 1+$\flat$3+ 5+6

Minor 6th Chords can by written with "**min6**" or "**–6**" following the name of the chord. For example: **Cmin6** or **C–6.**

TO FIND THE FORMULA:

Play the **Minor Chord** (**1st,** **lowered 3rd** and **5th**), and **add** the **6th** note of the scale to the chord.

Example: The **Cmin6** chord would be:	C	E$\flat$	G	A
	1	$\flat$3	5	6

SUSPENDED 4TH AND SUSPENDED 2ND CHORDS
FORMULA FOR SUSPENDED 4th CHORDS = 1+4+5
FORMULA FOR SUSPENDED 2nd CHORDS = 1+2+5

Suspended Chords can by written with **"sus"** and either **"4"** or **"2"** following the name of the chord. For example: **Csus4, Csus2, Csus**. There are both **Suspended 4th** and **Suspended 2nd** Chords. Often, these chords "resolve" to the Major Chord. In other words, they do not sound "final" and need another chord, preferably a Major Chord to follow it in order for it to sound final. **Note**: If there is no number after **"sus"**, then it is assumed that it is a **Suspended 4th**.

TO FIND THE FORMULAS:

For sus4 Chords:
Play the **1st**, **4th** and **5th** notes of the scale.

For sus2 Chords:
Play the **1st**, **2nd** and **5th** notes of the scale.

Example: The **Csus4** chord would be:	C	F	G
	1	4	5
Example: The **Csus2** chord would be:	C	D	G
	1	2	5

SUSPENDED 7TH CHORDS
FORMULA = 1+4+5+$^\flat$7

Suspended Chords can by written with **"sus7"** following the name of the chord. For example: Csus7. The Suspended 7th Chord adds the **lowered 7th** of the scale to the chord.

TO FIND THE FORMULA:

Play the **Suspended Chord** (**1st**, **4th** and **5th**) and add the **lowered 7th** note of the scale.

Example: The **Csus7** chord would be:	C	F	G	B$^\flat$
	1	4	5	$^\flat$7

MAJOR 7th, FLAT 5th CHORDS
FORMULA = $1+3+{}^\flat 5+7$

Major 7th, Flat 5th Chords can by written with "maj7$^\flat$5" or "M $^\flat$7" following the name of the chord. For example: **Cmaj7$^\flat$5** or **CM$^\flat$7**.

TO FIND THE FORMULA:

Play the **1st**, **3rd** and **lowered 5th** and **add** the **7th** note of the scale (**not lowered**) to the chord.

Example: The **Cmaj7$^\flat$5** chord would be:	C	E	G$^\flat$	B
	1	3	$^\flat$5	7

7th FLAT 5th CHORDS
FORMULA = $1+3+{}^\flat 5+{}^\flat 7$

7th, Flat 5th Chords can by written with "7$^\flat$5" following the name of the chord. For example: **C$^\flat$5**.

TO FIND THE FORMULA:

Play the **1st**, **3rd**, **lowered 5th** and **lowered 7th** note of the scale to the chord.

Example: The **C7$^\flat$5** chord would be:	C	E	G$^\flat$	B$^\flat$
	1	3	$^\flat$5	$^\flat$7

MINOR 7th, FLAT 5th CHORDS
(Half-diminished 7th chords)
FORMULA = 1+$\flat$3+$\flat$5+$\flat$7

Minor 7th, Flat 5th Chords (also known as "Half-diminished" chords) can by written with "min7$\flat$5" following the name of the chord. For example: **Cmin7$\flat$5**.

TO FIND THE FORMULA:

Play the **1st, lowered 3rd and lowered 5th** and **lowered 7th** note of the scale to the chord.

Example: The **Cmin7$\flat$5** chord would be:	C	E$\flat$	G$\flat$	B$\flat$
	1	$\flat$3	$\flat$5	$\flat$7

MINOR, MAJOR 7th CHORDS
FORMULA = 1+$\flat$3+5+7

Minor, Major7th Chords can by written with "min(M7)", "min/Maj7, or "— (maj7)" following the name of the chord. For example: **Cmin(M7), Cmin/Maj7** or **C—(maj7)**.

TO FIND THE FORMULA:

Play the **Minor Chord** (**1st, lowered 3rd** and **5th**), and **add** the **7th** note of the scale (**not lowered**) to the chord.

Example: The **Cmin/Maj7** chord would be:	C	E$\flat$	G	B
	1	$\flat$3	5	7

All 9th CHORDS

9th Chords can by written with **similar notations to the 7th Chords**. **9th Chords** are **split** between both left and right hands and often not all of the notes in each chord are played.

TO FIND THE FORMULAS:

Examples:

The **C9** chord would be:	C	E	G	B♭	D
	1	3	5	♭7	9
The **CMaj9** chord would be:	C	E	G	B	D
	1	3	5	7	9
The **Cmin9** chord would be:	C	E♭	G	B♭	D
	1	♭3	5	♭7	9
The **Cmin/Maj9** chord would be:	C	E♭	G	B	D
	1	♭3	5	7	9

All 11th CHORDS

11th Chords can by written with **similar notations to the 7th Chords**. **11th Chords** are **split** between both left and right hands and often not all of the notes in each chord are played.

TO FIND THE FORMULAS:

Examples:

The **C11** chord would be:	C	E	G	B♭	D	F
	1	3	5	♭7	9	11
The **CMaj11** chord would be:	C	E	G	B	D	F
	1	3	5	7	9	11
The **Cmin11** chord would be:	C	E♭	G	B♭	D	F
	1	♭3	5	♭7	9	11
The **Cmin/Maj11** chord would be:	C	E♭	G	B	D	F
	1	♭3	5	7	9	11

LESSON 24
BULDING OTHER TYPES OF CHORDS

All 13th CHORDS

11th Chords can by written with **similar notations to the 7th Chords.** **11th Chords** are **split** between both left and right hands and often not all of the notes in each chord are played.

Examples:

The **C13** chord would be:

	C	E	G	B♭	D	F	A
	1	3	5	♭7	9	11	13

The **CMaj13** chord would be:

	C	E	G	B	D	F	A
	1	3	5	7	9	11	13

The **Cmin13** chord would be:

	C	E♭	G	B♭	D	F	A
	1	♭3	5	♭7	9	11	13

The **Cmin/Maj13** chord would be:

	C	E♭	G	B	D	F	A
	1	♭3	5	7	9	11	13

"SLASH CHORDS"

A "Slash Chord" is actually just an inversion of any particular chord (see *Lesson 8, Chord Inversions*).

This is an example of what is called a "**Slash Chord**": **C/E.** This means that you should play the **C Chord** but with the **E as the bottom (lowest) note (or, in the bass).**

Example: The **C/E** slash chord would be played:

	E	G	C
	3	5	1

NOTES

HOW TO WRITE A SONG

In this lesson, you will learn how to write simple song, using the THREE MOST IMPORTANT CHORDS.

First of all, before we start, we want to determine a few things. These things are as follows:

1.   The Key Signature (what Key we are going to use)
2.   The Time Signature (how we want the song to feel)
3.   The Musical Form

We have already learned about Key Signatures, and you should know what time signatures are, such $\frac{4}{4}$ time, $\frac{3}{4}$ time, etc.

One thing you may not know about is Musical Form.

MUSICAL FORM

Musical Form is basically the "structure" of a piece of music – how it is formed. Music is basically made up of different "patterns" of sounds, or phrases. The Musical Form is the way that these phrases are put together. When talking about Musical Form, we use letters, such as A, B, and C. Let me give you an example:

If you have a song with the musical form of A-B-A-B, this means that the "A" sections sound basically the same, and the "B" sections sound basically the same. This could be a Verse-Chorus-Verse-Chorus type of song. Or, you might have a song made up of A-A-B-A, in which the "A" sections all sound similar, and the "B" section is entirely different. This is actually a very common type of musical form, and the type that we will be using in this lesson.

Let's get started!

SONG WRITING FRAME CHART

This sheet is our "Song Writing Frame Chart". I've created it to make it easier to "see" the song that you are going to write. We are going to write a simple 16 measure song.

In the first column, you will see the actual musical form and the letter section that we will be using, either "A", or "B".

In the second column, you will see the time signature. In this song we will be using $\frac{4}{4}$ time.

In the 3rd, 4th, 5th, and 6th columns you will see column headings, which will be used to place the "Chord Symbol" that you will want to use. Underneath these column headings is the space you will use to actually write in the notes to your song (the melody). (**See a completed Sample Song at the end of this lesson**.)

Form	Time signature	SONG				
A	$\frac{4}{4}$	**C** C E G E	A F A 2			← Chord symbols ← Melody ← Rhythm (type of note other than quarter note)
A	$\frac{4}{4}$					
B	$\frac{4}{4}$					
A	$\frac{4}{4}$				C	

WRITING YOUR SONG

When writing a song in a particular key, you will want to **START** the song with the root chord (1 chord) of that Key, and **END** the song with the root chord to that key. In this case, we are going to write our song in the Key of C, so the root chord would be C. It is already placed in the chart.

Since we are going to use the THREE MOST IMPORTANT CHORDS in the Key of C for this song, we will also be using the F Chord and the G Chord (the 4 and 5 chords in the Key of C).

You can write your song in one of two ways:

Method 1: Determine which chord you want to use in each measure and then figure out a melody according to that chord;

OR

Method 2: Determine your melody and then determine the chord you want to use in that measure.

To explain further, when writing a song, you need to keep in mind that whenever you want to change your CHORD, the melody note (for the most part – to keep it simple) should be in that chord.

Example (using Method 1): The first Chord of your song is the "C" Chord (see chart). Therefore, the melody in the first measure should have the notes that belong to the "C" Chord – either C, E, or G. (Now, this is very simplified, for teaching purposes. The first measure has been done for you). Notice that the C Chord is right above the first melody note, which is when you actually play the C Chord. These notes are all quarter notes.

Let's say that you choose to use the "F" Chord in the next measure. Write "F" in the measure next to the "C" and **choose notes from the F Chord** to create the melody in your 2nd measure.

Let's say that you choose to use the "G" Chord in the next measure. Write "G" in the next measure's chord box and **choose notes from the G Chord** to create the melody in your 3rd measure.

Complete the first line with any of these three chords and create a melody based on the notes in that chord.

Once you have completed the first line, repeat the same line in the next line, since it is also an "A" section.

Chord Piano Is Fun!

Once you come to the "B" section, mix up the chords, and create different patterns, such as half notes or eighth notes. For half notes, I would write a "2" under the note to indicated a half note, and for eighth notes, I would connect them with brackets (⊔). See the Sample Song following this lesson.

Once you complete the "B" section, repeat the "A" section to complete your song.

There, you've done it! Of course, this is quite simplified, and you can always add different notes that might sound good with each chord, as well as different types of notes, and you may want to make the last measure of one of the first two "A" sections a slight bit different, but for the most part they should be the same. Play around with sound and rhythm. Music always contains pattern, and our brains love to connect to pattern, so be sure to repeat your note patterns or rhythm patterns throughout the song to make it pleasurable to the hearer.

Example (using Method 2): The first chord of your song is the "C" Chord, so take off on that. Create a melody from the notes of this chord – using the C, E, or G notes. From there, you may "hear" a melody in your head, and want to pick it out on the piano. Once you have a measure that you like, write the notes down. THEN, determine which chord to play at the beginning of the measure. For example, If the melody of the next measure begins with the "A" note, determine which of the C, F, or G chord has an "A" in it. It would be the F Chord. Put "F" above the melody line. Do the same with the next measure. If the measure begins with the G", determine which chord has a G in it – it would be either C or G. Try both of these chords and see what sounds best to your ear. Write that chord above the melody. Continue this for the first line.

Once you have completed the first line, repeat the same line in the next line, since it is also an "A" section.

Once you come to the "B" section, start with a different melody line altogether, and match the chord to the notes. Try to create different patterns, such as half notes or eighth notes. For half notes, I would write a "2" under the note to indicated a half note, and for eighth notes, I would connect them with brackets (see example following this lesson).

Once you complete the "B" section, repeat the "A" section to complete your song.

There, you've done it! Of course, this is quite simplified, and you can always put more than one chord in each measure, if you would like. You may want to make the last measure of one of the first two "A" sections a slight bit different, but for the most part they should be the same. Play around with sound and rhythm. Music always contains pattern, and our brains love to connect to pattern, so be sure to repeat your note patterns or rhythm patterns throughout the song to make it pleasurable to the hearer.

After you have written your song, NAME IT! Give yourself time to think of a good name – one that fits the song. If you have a good notation software program, such as capella (**www.capella-software.com** – it's free) recreate your song so that it actually looks like music. Have fun! This is your song!

Sample Song

Breezeway

A	4/4	C	F	G	F	← Chord symbols
		C E G E	A F A 2 ↑ (indicates half note)	G D B D	F A F 2	← Melody ← Rhythm (type of note other than quarter note)
A	4/4	C C E G E	F A F A 2	G G D B D	C G E C 2	
B	4/4	F F A F A F A ⊔ ⊔ ⊔ ⊔ ↗ ↖ (indicates eighth notes)	G D G D G D G D G ⊔ ⊔ ⊔ ⊔	F F A F A F A ⊔ ⊔ ⊔ ⊔	G G D B D G ⊔ ⊔ 2	
A	4/4	C C E G E	F A F A 2	G G D B D	C G E C 2	

Notice that the half notes have a "2' written under them, and the 8ᵗʰ notes are connected with brackets (⊔).

You can use this formula/chart with any key, either Major or Minor. Next time, try a song in A minor to hear the difference in the sound! Just use the THREE MOST IMPORTANT CHORDS in this key.

Another song you write might also include those family chords other than the THREE MOST IMPORTANT CHORDS. Be creative and have fun!

ADDITIONAL SONG-WRITING FRAME CHART

Form	Time signature	SONG			

PLAYING THE BLUES

In this lesson, you will learn how to "play the Blues!" The "Blues" is type of music genre which has a very distinct sound, which most people find appealing, and which is a lot of fun. The Blues are made up of three elements:

- Blues Scale
- Blues Chords
- Blues Form.

THE BLUES SCALE

A "**BLUES SCALE**" is another type of scale that can be used when playing music, and what are often used when playing blues or jazz.

The Blues Scales consists of the following notes from the Major Scale:

1, $^\flat$3, 4, $^\flat$5, 5, and $^\flat$7

For example, in the Key of C, these notes would be:

C, E$^\flat$, F, G$^\flat$, G, and B$^\flat$.

This is the fingering I use for the Blues Scale in the Key of C:

Key of C

All other keys and their fingerings can be found in **Addendum 6 – Blues Scales.**

Chord Piano Is Fun!

BLUES CHORDS

The typical "Blues Chords" consist of the I^7, IV^7 and V^7 Chords.

> **For example, in the Key of C, these chords would be:**
>
> C^7, F^7 and G^7

BLUES FORM

The typical "Blues Form" consists of the following form:

4 bars (measures) of the I^7 Chord
2 bars of the IV^7 Chord
2 Bars of the I^7 chord
1 bar of the V^7 Chord
1 bar of the IV^7 Chord
2 bars of the I^7 Chord

For example, in the Key of C, this would be:

Number of Bars	Chord
4	C^7
2	F^7
2	C^7
1	G^7
1	F^7
2	C^7

This is called the "12 Bar Blues". There are other variations of the 12 Bar Blues, but this is one of the most popular.

HOW TO PLAY THE BLUES

Try making up a Blues Song doing the following:

With your left hand, play the **Blues Chord** indicated in each bar of the above **Blues Form**.

While playing these chords, improvise a melody with your right hand by just playing the notes in the **Key of C Blues Scale.**   You can use any of the notes in the Blues Scale, in any order while you are playing each chord.

BE SURE that you are **counting 4 BEATS TO EACH MEASURE and change the chord according to the Blues Form.**

Make sure that you count See how it sounds! Try different rhythms to make it sound even better. You are on your way to being a "Blues Master!"

You can also try this in different keys (see **Addendum 6 – Blues Scales**).

NOTES

Use this page to write out the notes and chords you would use for the key of G and the Key of F. Try a song in these key signatures as well! See how you do!

Chord Piano Is Fun!

ACCOMPANYING YOURSELF OR OTHERS

Accompanying a singer is a bit different than the way we have been learning. However, the chord concepts are the same.

When you accompany a singer, you do not play the melody notes with your right hand. Instead, **you typically play the chord with either just your right hand, or broken up between both hands.** The melody of the song will be covered by the singer.

In addition to playing the chords this way, you will also add "rhythm patterns" to the chords to add interest.

"Chord sheets" are written with ONLY the words of the song and the chords written above the word where the chord changes. Many worship songs are written this way. The piano (as well as guitars, etc.) play the chords written, while the singers sing the melody.

Here are a few examples of simple "**Accompaniment Patterns**" that you can try with some of your favorite songs:

Simple Accompaniment Pattern 1

Instead of using chords in your **left** hand, you will use the chords in your **right** hand and your left hand will be playing a bass note.

- The bass note you use in your left hand is the **ROOT NOTE** of the chord you are playing. The melody of the song is being covered by the singer.

- The rhythm you are using in the right hand is just simple **quarter notes**. Keep the rhythm even, playing quarter notes for each beat of the measure.

Try this with the following "chord sheet":

On Top of Old Smoky (3/4 time)

```
    C        F
On top of Old Smokey
               C
All covered with snow,
          G
I lost my true lover
              C    F   C
For courting too slow.
```

You can also use the above accompaniment pattern for songs such as:

Hey Jude (Beatles)
Hallelujah (Rufus Wainwright – from "Shrek")
Let It Be (Beatles)
I Can Only Imagine (Mercy Me)
And many others!

> **You can find a video examples of these patterns at my website (www.chordpianoisfun.com). Go to "Instructional Videos".**

Simple Accompaniment Pattern 2

This simple accompaniment pattern can be used for Christmas music or other ballads. I personally love the sound of this pattern.

This pattern consists of playing the root note of the chord with the left hand, and the chord written with the right hand, but you will be **adding the 2nd** to the chord. You will play the 2,3, and 5 together and then moving to the 1 (root) in an 8th note pattern. Try this with "**Away In A Manger.**"

Away In A Manger (3/4 time)

```
  C              F        C
Away in a manger, no crib for a bed,

  G              F          C
The little Lord Jesus lay down His sweet head,

   C             F          C
The stars in the sky look down where he lay,

  G      C      F     G C
The little Lord Jesus, asleep on the hay.
```

These are just a few examples of accompaniment patterns, which can be used for many different kinds of songs. Please check my website for updates and additions.

EPILOGUE

WHAT NOW?

NOTES

Chord Piano Is Fun!

EPILOGUE

WHAT NOW?

You have just completed **CHORD PIANO IS FUN**, and I hope that you learned a great deal and your musical world has been expanded!

As a customer, you have **free access** to updates, additions, news, new music, and videos to **Chord Piano Is Fun!** as they become available. Go to the **CUSTOMER PAGE** at www.chordpianoisfun.com and sign in using the login **cpifcustomer**. Also be sure to sign up for the **NEWSLETTER** so you can be informed of any additions.

The fun part about learning **chord piano** is that you can do so much with it. I would encourage you to pick up any popular music that you like at the music store that has **chord symbols**, and start playing the chords in the book with your left hand along with the right hand notes. You may also want to pick up a **"Fake Book"**. There are several Fake Books on the market and they show the right hand notes and the chord symbol, much like I have done in this book. (For some great Fake Books, you can go to *http://tiny.cc/ulkuz*.) You can use just **block chords**, or you can try to **break the chord up** in rhythm with the song to make the song more interesting.

If you want to **accompany a singer (including yourself)**, you can also play the **root note** of the chord with your **left hand** (in the bass – below middle C) and the **chord** in your **right**. This is typically how this is done when you are accompanying yourself as a singer or someone else. I think you'll be amazed at how much you have learned so far!!!

I would also recommend review all of the **ADDENDUMS ("CHORD STUFF")** following this page. Practice going through your **SCALES**, and your **MOST IMPORTANT CHORDS** for each **KEY**. These will be instrumental in keeping your mind SHARP when it comes to chords, and when you play from chord charts these chords will come naturally. Be sure to practice your chords according to the instructions in *Lesson 8* and *Lesson 12*.

As I stated in the forward of this book, this by no means is a complete, exhaustive composite of all that you can learn about **chord piano**. So, I don't want to leave you hanging if you want more. If you would like more information or training regarding chord patterns which would add more "oomph" to your chords and right or left hand, please go to **Scott Houston's** website, *www.scotthouston.com*. He has wonderful videos on tricks of the trade, as well as other books on chording patterns, etc. Another method which will show you how to progress with your chords is **ProProach:** *http://bit.ly/esaMjh*

I hope you've enjoyed **CHORD PIANO IS FUN!** and that you found that is was worth the small price that you paid!

Thank you again, and God bless,

T. K. Goforth

NOTES

Chord Piano Is Fun!

CHORD STUFF
(ADDENDUMS)

NOTES

ADDENDUM 1

MAJOR AND MINOR SCALES

(With Family Chords)

NOTES

Chord Piano Is Fun!

MAJOR AND MINOR SCALES

MAJOR SCALES

Major Scales are the scales which most of music is built around. These are the most common scales. These scales have a certain quality, which makes them sound "**happy**" or "**pleasant**."

MINOR SCALES

Minor scales have a certain quality, which makes them sound somewhat "**sad**". Many songs are written based on these minor scales, just as many songs **are based on the notes in the Major Scales. Each Major Scale has a RELATIVE MINOR SCALE.**

RELATIVE MINOR SCALES

Each Major Scale has what is called the "**RELATIVE MINOR SCALE**" that contains the same number of sharps or flats in its Key Signature. It is called the "Relative Minor" scale because it is "a relative" of the Major Scale – it has the same Key Signature. For example, the C Major Scale has NO sharps or flats, and the A Minor Scale also has no sharps or flats. So, the A Minor Scale is called the "Relative Minor Scale" of the C Major Scale.

To find the **Relative Minor Scale** of a particular Major Scale, find the first note of the Major Scale and **go down 1 ½ steps** on the piano. This is the first note of the Relative Minor Scale and it will use the same Key Signature as its Relative Major Scale.

There are **3 TYPES** of Minor Scales:

TYPES OF MINOR SCALES

The Relative Minor Scale can be **adjusted** depending on the type of sound that wants to be obtained. Or, it can just be left "as is" – meaning containing the exact same notes as it's Relative Major Scale. Because of this, there are three different **TYPES** of Minor Scales:

NATURAL MINOR SCALE (RELATIVE MINOR)

When you play the Relative Minor Scale with **no adjustments,** and use the exact same notes as its Relative Major Scale this is called the **NATURAL MINOR SCALE.** For example: The A Natural Minor Scale contains the **same notes** as the C Major Scale, except that the scale starts on "A".

There are two other Minor Scales, and these notes DO have adjustments made to the notes in the scale:

HARMONIC MINOR SCALE

In the **HARMONIC MINOR SCALE,** the **7th** note of the scale is **RAISED ½ STEP** both **ascending** and **descending** the scale.

MELODIC MINOR SCALE

In the **MELODIC MINOR SCALE,** both the **6th** and **7th** notes of the scale are **RAISED ½ STEP** as you **ascend** the scale, but while **descending** the scale you **return to the Natural Minor** (Relative Minor) Scale.

SCALES
NO SHARPS OR FLATS

C MAJOR SCALE = NO SHARPS OF FLATS

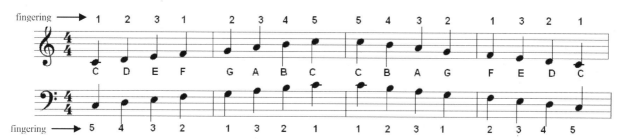

NOTES OF THE SCALE:	C	D	E	F	G	A	B	C
DEGREES OF THE SCALE:	1	2	3	4	5	6	7	8
TECHNICAL NAMES :	Tonic	Super-tonic	Mediant	Sub-dominant	Dominant	Sub-mediant	Leading Tone	Tonic
FAMILY CHORDS: (Most Important HIGHLIGHTED):	C (I)	Dm (ii)	Em (iii)	F (IV)	G or G7 (V or V7)	Am (vi)	Bdim (vii°)	

A NATURAL MINOR SCALE (Relative of C Major) = NO SHARPS OR FLATS

NOTES OF THE SCALE:	A	B	C	D	A	F	G	D
DEGREES OF THE SCALE:	1	2	3	4	5	6	7	8
TECHNICAL NAMES :	Tonic	Super-tonic	Mediant	Sub-dominant	Dominant	Sub-mediant	Leading Tone	Tonic
FAMILY CHORDS: (Most Important HIGHLIGHTED):	Am (i)	Bdim (ii°)	C (III)	Dm (iv)	Em, E, or E7 (v, V, or V7)	F (VI)	G (VII)	

A HARMONIC MINOR SCALE
RAISE the 7th note of the scale ½ STEP both **ascending** and **descending** the scale.

A MELODIC MINOR SCALE
RAISE both the 6th and 7th notes of the scale ½ STEP as you **ascend** the scale, but while **descending** the scale return to the **Natural Minor Scale**.

SHARP SCALES
NOTE THE ORDER OF SHARPS ADDED TO EACH SCALE – F C G D E A B

G MAJOR SCALE = 1 SHARP = F#

NOTES OF THE SCALE:	G	A	B	C	D	E	F	G
DEGREES OF THE SCALE:	1	2	3	4	5	6	7	8
TECHNICAL NAMES:	Tonic	Super-tonic	Mediant	Sub-dominant	Dominant	Sub-mediant	Leading Tone	Tonic
FAMILY CHORDS: (Most Important HIGHLIGHTED):	G (I)	Am (ii)	Bm (iii)	C (IV)	D or D7 (V or V7)	Em (vi)	F#dim (vii°)	

E NATURAL MINOR SCALE (Relative of G Major) = 1 SHARP = F#

NOTES OF THE SCALE:	E	F	G	A	B	C	D	E
DEGREES OF THE SCALE:	1	2	3	4	5	6	7	8
TECHNICAL NAMES:	Tonic	Super-tonic	Mediant	Sub-dominant	Dominant	Sub-mediant	Leading Tone	Tonic
FAMILY CHORDS: (Most Important HIGHLIGHTED):	Em (i)	F#dim (ii°)	G (III)	Am (iv)	Bm, B, or B7 (v, V, or V7)	C (VI)	D (VII)	

E HARMONIC MINOR SCALE
RAISE the 7th note of the scale ½ STEP both **ascending** and **descending** the scale.

E MELODIC MINOR SCALE
RAISE both the **6th** and **7th** notes of the scale ½ STEP as you **ascend** the scale, but while **descending** the scale return to the **Natural Minor Scale.**

D MAJOR SCALE = 2 SHARPS = F#, C#

NOTES OF THE SCALE:	D	E	F#	G	A	B	C#	D
DEGREES OF THE SCALE:	1	2	3	4	5	6	7	8
TECHNICAL NAMES:	Tonic	Super-tonic	Mediant	Sub-dominant	Dominant	Sub-mediant	Leading Tone	Tonic
FAMILY CHORDS: (Most Important HIGHLIGHTED):	D (I)	Em (ii)	F#m (iii)	G (IV)	A or A7 (V or V7)	Bm (vi)	C#dim (vii°)	

B NATURAL MINOR SCALE (Relative of D Major) = 2 SHARPS = F#, C#

NOTES OF THE SCALE:	B	C#	D	E	F#	G	A	B
DEGREES OF THE SCALE:	1	2	3	4	5	6	7	8
TECHNICAL NAMES:	Tonic	Super-tonic	Mediant	Sub-dominant	Dominant	Sub-mediant	Leading Tone	Tonic
FAMILY CHORDS: (Most Important HIGHLIGHTED):	Bm (i)	C#dim (ii°)	D (III)	Em (iv)	F#m, F#, or F#7 (v, V, or V7)	G (VI)	A (VII)	

B HARMONIC MINOR SCALE:
RAISE the **7th** note of the scale ½ STEP both **ascending** and **descending** the scale.

B MELODIC MINOR SCALE:
RAISE both the **6th** and **7th** notes of the scale ½ STEP as you **ascend** the scale, but while **descending** the scale return to the **Natural Minor Scale**.

ADDENDUM 1
MAJOR AND MINOR SCALES

A MAJOR SCALE = 3 SHARPS = F#, C#, G#

NOTES OF THE SCALE:	A	B	C#	D	E	F#	G#	A
DEGREES OF THE SCALE:	1	2	3	4	5	6	7	8
TECHNICAL NAMES:	Tonic	Super-tonic	Mediant	Sub-dominant	Dominant	Sub-mediant	Leading Tone	Tonic
FAMILY CHORDS:	A	Bm	C#m	D	E or E7	F#m	G#dim	
(Most Important HIGHLIGHTED):	(I)	(ii)	(iii)	(IV)	(V or V7)	(vi)	(vii°)	

F# NATURAL MINOR SCALE (Relative of A Major) = 3 SHARPS = F#, C#, G#

NOTES OF THE SCALE:	F	G	A	B	C#	D	E	F
DEGREES OF THE SCALE:	1	2	3	4	5	6	7	8
TECHNICAL NAMES:	Tonic	Super-tonic	Mediant	Sub-dominant	Dominant	Sub-mediant	Leading Tone	Tonic
FAMILY CHORDS:	Fm	G#dim	A	Bm	C#m, C#, or C#7	D	E	
(Most Important HIGHLIGHTED):	(i)	(ii°)	(III)	(iv)	(v, V, or V7)	(VI)	(VII)	

F# HARMONIC MINOR SCALE
RAISE the **7**th note of the scale ½ STEP both **ascending** and **descending** the scale.

F# MELODIC MINOR SCALE
RAISE both the **6th** and **7th** notes of the scale ½ STEP as you **ascend** the scale, but while **descending** the scale return to the **Natural Minor Scale**.

E MAJOR SCALE = 4 SHARPS = F#, C#, G#, D#

NOTES OF THE SCALE:	E	F#	G#	A	B	C#	D#	E
DEGREES OF THE SCALE:	1	2	3	4	5	6	7	8
TECHNICAL NAMES:	Tonic	Super-tonic	Mediant	Sub-dominant	Dominant	Sub-mediant	Leading Tone	Tonic
FAMILY CHORDS:	E	F#m	G#m	A	B or B7	C#m	D#dim	
(Most Important HIGHLIGHTED):	(I)	(ii)	(iii)	(IV)	(V or V7)	(vi)	(vii°)	

C# NATURAL MINOR SCALE (Relative of E Major) = 4 SHARPS = F#, C#, G#, D#

NOTES OF THE SCALE:	C#	D#	E	F#	G#	A	B	C#
DEGREES OF THE SCALE:	1	2	3	4	5	6	7	8
TECHNICAL NAMES:	Tonic	Super-tonic	Mediant	Sub-dominant	Dominant	Sub-mediant	Leading Tone	Tonic
FAMILY CHORDS:	C#m	D#dim	E	F#m	G#m, G#, or G#7	A	B	
(Most Important HIGHLIGHTED):	(i)	(ii°)	(III)	(iv)	(v, V, or V7)	(VI)	(VII)	

C# HARMONIC MINOR SCALE
RAISE the **7th** note of the scale ½ STEP both **ascending** and **descending** the scale.

C# MELODIC MINOR SCALE
RAISE both the **6th** and **7th** notes of the scale ½ STEP as you **ascend** the scale, but while **descending** the scale return to the **Natural Minor Scale**.

ADDENDUM 1
MAJOR AND MINOR SCALES

B MAJOR SCALE = 5 SHARPS = F#, C#, G#, D#, A#

(The B Major Scale uses the same notes as the C♭ Major Scale – "Enharmonic")

NOTES OF THE SCALE:	B	C#	D#	E	F#	G#	A#	B
DEGREES OF THE SCALE:	1	2	3	4	5	6	7	8
TECHNICAL NAMES:	Tonic	Super-tonic	Mediant	Sub-dominant	Dominant	Sub-mediant	Leading Tone	Tonic
FAMILY CHORDS:	B	C#m	D#m	E	F# or F#7	G#m	A#dim	
Most Important HIGHLIGHTED):	(I)	(ii)	(iii)	(IV)	(V or V7)	(vi)	(vii°)	

G# NATURAL MINOR SCALE (Relative of B Major) = 5 SHARPS = F#, C#, G#, D#, A# (The G# Natural Scale uses the same notes as the A♭ Minor Scale – "Enharmonic")

NOTES OF THE SCALE:	G#	A#	B	C#	D#	E	F#	G#
DEGREES OF THE SCALE:	1	2	3	4	5	6	7	8
TECHNICAL NAMES:	Tonic	Super-tonic	Mediant	Sub-dominant	Dominant	Sub-mediant	Leading Tone	Tonic
FAMILY CHORDS:	G#m	A#dim	B	C#m	D#m, D#, or D#7	E	F#	
(Most Important HIGHLIGHTED):	(i)	(ii°)	(III)	(iv)	(v, V. or V7)	(VI)	(VII)	

G# HARMONIC MINOR SCALE:
RAISE the **7**[th] note of the scale ½ **STEP** both **ascending** and **descending** the scale.

G# MELODIC MINOR SCALE:
RAISE both the **6th** and **7th** notes of the scale ½ **STEP** as you **ascend** the scale, but while **descending** the scale return to the **Natural Minor Scale.**

F# MAJOR SCALE = 6 SHARPS = F#, C#, G#, D#, A#, E#

(the F# Major Scale uses the same notes as the G♭ Major Scale – "Enharmonic")

NOTES OF THE SCALE:	F#	G#	A#	B	C#	D#	E#	F#
DEGREES OF THE SCALE:	1	2	3	4	5	6	7	8
TECHNICAL NAMES:	Tonic	Super-tonic	Mediant	Sub-dominant	Dominant	Sub-mediant	Leading Tone	Tonic
FAMILY CHORDS:	F#	G#m	A#m	B	C# or C#7	D#m	E#dim	
(Most Important HIGHLIGHTED):	(I)	(ii)	(iii)	(IV)	(V or V7)	(vi)	(vii°)	

D# NATURAL MINOR SCALE (Relative of F# Major) = 6 SHARPS = F#, C#, G#, D#, A#, E#

NOTES OF THE SCALE:	D#	E#	F#	G#	A#	B	C#	D#
DEGREES OF THE SCALE:	1	2	3	4	5	6	7	8
TECHNICAL NAMES:	Tonic	Super-tonic	Mediant	Sub-dominant	Dominant	Sub-mediant	Leading Tone	Tonic
FAMILY CHORDS:	D#m	E#dim	F#	G#m	A#m, A#, or A#7	B	C#	
(Most Important HIGHLIGHTED):	(i)	(ii°)	(III)	(iv)	(v, V, or V7)	(VI)	(VII)	

D# HARMONIC MINOR SCALE

RAISE the <u>7th</u> note of the scale ½ STEP both **ascending** and **descending** the scale.

D# MELODIC MINOR SCALE

RAISE both the <u>6th</u> and <u>7th</u> notes of the scale ½ STEP as you **ascend** the scale, but while **descending** the scale <u>return to the **Natural Minor Scale**</u>.

C# MAJOR SCALE = 7 SHARPS = F#, C#, G#, D#, A#, E#, B#
(the C# Major Scale uses the same notes as the D♭ Major Scale – "Enharmonic")

NOTES OF THE SCALE:	C#	D#	E#	F#	G#	A#	B#	C#
DEGREES OF THE SCALE:	1	2	3	4	5	6	7	8
TECHNICAL NAMES:	Tonic	Super-tonic	Mediant	Sub-dominant	Dominant	Sub-mediant	Leading Tone	Tonic
FAMILY CHORDS:	C#	D#m	E#m	F#	G# or G#7	A#m	B#dim	
(Most Important HIGHLIGHTED):	(I)	(ii)	(iii)	(IV)	(V or V7)	(vi)	(vii°)	

A# NATURAL MINOR SCALE (Relative of F# Major) = 7 SHARPS = F#, C#, G#, D#, A#, E#, B# (the A# Minor Scale uses the same notes as the B♭ Minor Scale – "Enharmonic")

NOTES OF THE SCALE:	A#	B#	C#	D#	E#	F#	G#	A#
DEGREES OF THE SCALE:	1	2	3	4	5	6	7	8
TECHNICAL NAMES:	Tonic	Super-tonic	Mediant	Sub-dominant	Dominant	Sub-mediant	Leading Tone	Tonic
FAMILY CHORDS:	A#m	B#dim	C#	D#m	E#m, E#, or E#7	F#	G#	
(Most Important HIGHLIGHTED):	(i)	(ii°)	(III)	(iv)	(v, V, or V7)	(VI)	(VII)	

A# HARMONIC MINOR SCALE
RAISE the **7th** note of the scale ½ STEP both **ascending** and **descending** the scale.

A# MELODIC MINOR SCALE
RAISE both the **6th** and **7th** notes of the scale ½ STEP as you **ascend** the scale, but while **descending** the scale return to the **Natural Minor Scale**.

FLAT SCALES
NOTE THE ORDER OF FLATS ADDED: B E A D G C F

F MAJOR SCALE = 1 FLAT = B♭

NOTES OF THE SCALE:	F	G	A	B♭	C	D	E	F
DEGREES OF THE SCALE:	1	2	3	4	5	6	7	8
TECHNICAL NAMES:	Tonic	Super-tonic	Mediant	Sub-dominant	Dominant	Sub-mediant	Leading Tone	Tonic
FAMILY CHORDS:	F	Gm	Am	B♭	C or C7	Dm	Edim	
(Most Important HIGHLIGHTED):	(I)	(ii)	(iii)	(IV)	(V or V7)	(vi)	(vii°)	

D NATURAL MINOR SCALE (Relative of F Major) = 1 FLAT = B♭

NOTES OF THE SCALE:	D	E	F	G	A	B♭	C	D
DEGREES OF THE SCALE:	1	2	3	4	5	6	7	8
TECHNICAL NAMES:	Tonic	Super-tonic	Mediant	Sub-dominant	Dominant	Sub-mediant	Leading Tone	Tonic
FAMILY CHORDS:	Dm	Edim	F	Gm	Am, A, or A7	B♭	C	
(Most Important HIGHLIGHTED):	(i)	(ii°)	(III)	(iv)	(v, V, or V7)	(VI)	(VII)	

D HARMONIC MINOR SCALE:
RAISE the 7th note of the scale ½ STEP both **ascending** and **descending** the scale.

D MELODIC MINOR SCALE:
RAISE both the 6th and 7th notes of the scale ½ STEP as you **ascend** the scale, but while **descending** the scale return to the **Natural Minor Scale**.

ADDENDUM 1
MAJOR AND MINOR SCALES

B♭ MAJOR SCALE = 2 FLATS = B♭, E♭

NOTES OF THE SCALE:	B♭	C	D	E♭	F	G	A	Bb
DEGREES OF THE SCALE:	1	2	3	4	5	6	7	8
TECHNICAL NAMES:	Tonic	Super-tonic	Mediant	Sub-dominant	Dominant	Sub-mediant	Leading Tone	Tonic
FAMILY CHORDS:	B♭	Cm	Dm	E♭	F or F7	Gm	Adim	
(Most Important HIGHLIGHTED):	(I)	(ii)	(iii)	(IV)	(V or V7)	(vi)	(vii°)	

G NATURAL MINOR SCALE (Relative of B♭ Major) = 2 FLATS = B♭, E♭

NOTES OF THE SCALE:	G	A	B♭	C	Dm	E♭	F	G
DEGREES OF THE SCALE:	1	2	3	4	5	6	7	8
TECHNICAL NAMES:	Tonic	Super-tonic	Mediant	Sub-dominant	Dominant	Sub-mediant	Leading Tone	Tonic
FAMILY CHORDS:	Gm	Adim	B♭	Cm	Dm, D, or D7	E♭	F	
(Most Important HIGHLIGHTED):	(i)	(ii°)	(III)	(iv)	(v, V, or V7)	(VI)	(VII)	

G HARMONIC MINOR SCALE:
RAISE the **7**[th] note of the scale ½ STEP both **ascending** and **descending** the scale.

G MELODIC MINOR SCALE:
RAISE both the **6th** and **7th** notes of the scale ½ STEP as you **ascend** the scale, but while **descending** the scale return to the **Natural Minor Scale**.

E♭ MAJOR SCALE = 3 FLATS = B♭, E♭, A♭

NOTES OF THE SCALE:	E♭	F	G	A♭	B♭	C	D	E♭
DEGREES OF THE SCALE:	1	2	3	4	5	6	7	8
TECHNICAL NAMES:	Tonic	Super-tonic	Mediant	Sub-dominant	Dominant	Sub-mediant	Leading Tone	Tonic
FAMILY CHORDS:	E♭	Fm	Gm	A♭	B♭ or B♭7	Cm	Ddim	
(Most Important HIGHLIGHTED):	(I)	(ii)	(iii)	(IV)	(V or V7)	(vi)	(vii°)	

C NATURAL MINOR SCALE (Relative of E♭ Major) = 3 FLATS = B♭, E♭,

NOTES OF THE SCALE:	C	D	E♭	F	Gm	A♭	B♭	C
DEGREES OF THE SCALE:	1	2	3	4	5	6	7	8
TECHNICAL NAMES:	Tonic	Super-tonic	Mediant	Sub-dominant	Dominant	Sub-mediant	Leading Tone	Tonic
FAMILY CHORDS:	Cm	Ddim	E♭	Fm	Gm, G, or G7	A♭	B♭	
(Most Important HIGHLIGHTED):	(i)	(ii°)	(III)	(iv)	(v, V, or V7)	(VI)	(VII)	

C HARMONIC MINOR SCALE:
RAISE the <u>7th</u> note of the scale ½ STEP both **ascending** and **descending** the scale.

C MELODIC MINOR SCALE:
RAISE both the **6th** and **7th** notes of the scale ½ STEP as you **ascend** the scale, but while **descending** the scale <u>return to the **Natural Minor Scale**</u>.

A♭ MAJOR SCALE = 4 FLATS = B♭, E♭, A♭, D♭

NOTES OF THE SCALE:	A♭	B♭	C	D♭	E♭	F	G	A♭
DEGREES OF THE SCALE:	1	2	3	4	5	6	7	8
TECHNICAL NAMES:	Tonic	Super-tonic	Mediant	Sub-dominant	Dominant	Sub-mediant	Leading Tone	Tonic
FAMILY CHORDS: (Most Important HIGHLIGHTED):	A♭ (I)	B♭m (ii)	Cm (iii)	D♭ (IV)	E♭ or E♭7 (V or V7)	Fm (vi)	Gdim (vii°)	

F NATURAL MINOR SCALE (Relative of A♭ Major) = 4 FLATS = B♭, E♭, A♭, D♭

NOTES OF THE SCALE:	F	G	A♭	B♭	Cm	D♭	E♭	F
DEGREES OF THE SCALE:	1	2	3	4	5	6	7	8
TECHNICAL NAMES:	Tonic	Super-tonic	Mediant	Sub-dominant	Dominant	Sub-mediant	Leading Tone	Tonic
FAMILY CHORDS: (Most Important HIGHLIGHTED):	Fm (i)	Gdim (ii°)	A♭ (III)	B♭m (iv)	Cm, C, or C7 (v, V, or V7)	D♭ (VI)	E♭ (VII)	

F HARMONIC MINOR SCALE:
RAISE the <u>7th</u> note of the scale ½ STEP both **ascending** and **descending** the scale.

F MELODIC MINOR SCALE:
RAISE both the <u>6th</u> and <u>7th</u> notes of the scale ½ STEP as you **ascend** the scale, but while **descending** the scale <u>return to the **Natural Minor Scale**</u>.

D♭ MAJOR SCALE = 5 FLATS = B♭, E♭, A♭, D♭, G♭

(the D♭ Major Scale uses the same notes as the C# Major Scale – "Enharmonic")

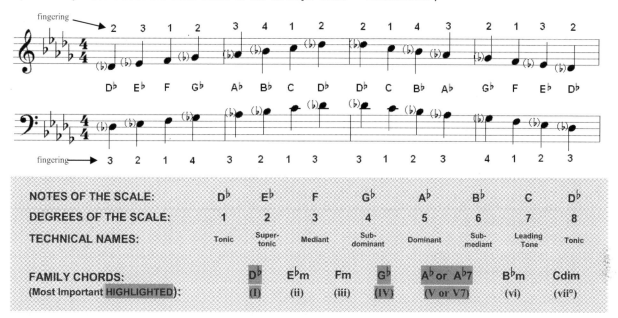

NOTES OF THE SCALE:	D♭	E♭	F	G♭	A♭	B♭	C	D♭
DEGREES OF THE SCALE:	1	2	3	4	5	6	7	8
TECHNICAL NAMES:	Tonic	Super-tonic	Mediant	Sub-dominant	Dominant	Sub-mediant	Leading Tone	Tonic
FAMILY CHORDS: (Most Important HIGHLIGHTED):	D♭ (I)	E♭m (ii)	Fm (iii)	G♭ (IV)	A♭ or A♭7 (V or V7)	B♭m (vi)	Cdim (vii°)	

B♭ NATURAL MINOR SCALE (Relative of D♭ Major) = 5 FLATS = B♭, E♭,

A♭, D♭, G♭ (the B♭ Minor Scale uses the same notes as the A# Minor Scale – "Enharmonic")

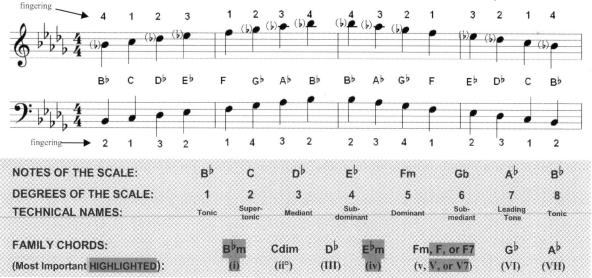

NOTES OF THE SCALE:	B♭	C	D♭	E♭	Fm	Gb	A♭	B♭
DEGREES OF THE SCALE:	1	2	3	4	5	6	7	8
TECHNICAL NAMES:	Tonic	Super-tonic	Mediant	Sub-dominant	Dominant	Sub-mediant	Leading Tone	Tonic
FAMILY CHORDS: (Most Important HIGHLIGHTED):	B♭m (i)	Cdim (ii°)	D♭ (III)	E♭m (iv)	Fm, F, or F7 (v, V, or V7)	G♭ (VI)	A♭ (VII)	

B♭ HARMONIC MINOR SCALE:

RAISE the **7th** note of the scale ½ STEP both **ascending** and **descending** the scale.

B♭ MELODIC MINOR SCALE:

RAISE both the **6th** and **7th** notes of the scale ½ STEP as you **ascend** the scale, but while **descending** the scale return to the **Natural Minor Scale**.

ADDENDUM 1
MAJOR AND MINOR SCALES

G♭ MAJOR SCALE = 6 FLATS = B♭, E♭, A♭, D♭, G♭, C♭

(the G♭ Major Scale uses the same notes as the F# Major Scale – "Enharmonic")

NOTES OF THE SCALE:	G♭	A♭	B♭	C♭	D♭	E♭	F	G♭
DEGREES OF THE SCALE:	1	2	3	4	5	6	7	8
TECHNICAL NAMES:	Tonic	Super-tonic	Mediant	Sub-dominant	Dominant	Sub-mediant	Leading Tone	Tonic
FAMILY CHORDS:	G♭	A♭m	B♭m	C♭	D♭ or D♭7	E♭m	Fdim	
(Most Important HIGHLIGHTED):	(I)	(ii)	(iii)	(IV)	(V or V7)	(vi)	(vii°)	

E♭ NATURAL MINOR SCALE (Relative of G♭ Major) = 6 FLATS = B♭, E♭, A♭, D♭, G♭, C♭ (The E♭ Major Scale uses the same notes as the D# Minor Scale – "Enharmonic")

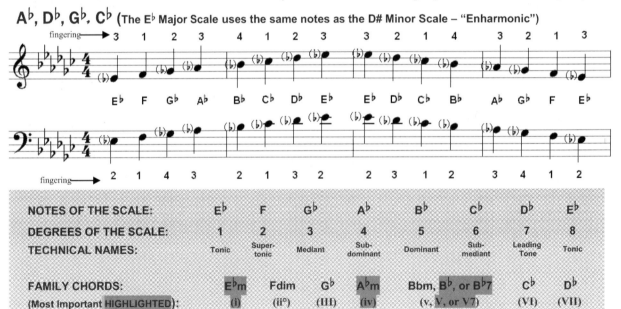

NOTES OF THE SCALE:	E♭	F	G♭	A♭	B♭	C♭	D♭	E♭
DEGREES OF THE SCALE:	1	2	3	4	5	6	7	8
TECHNICAL NAMES:	Tonic	Super-tonic	Mediant	Sub-dominant	Dominant	Sub-mediant	Leading Tone	Tonic
FAMILY CHORDS:	E♭m	Fdim	G♭	A♭m	Bbm, B♭, or B♭7	C♭	D♭	
(Most Important HIGHLIGHTED):	(i)	(ii°)	(III)	(iv)	(v, V, or V7)	(VI)	(VII)	

E♭ HARMONIC MINOR SCALE:
RAISE the **7th** note of the scale ½ **STEP** both **ascending** and **descending** the scale.

E♭ MELODIC MINOR SCALE:
RAISE both the **6th** and **7th** notes of the scale ½ **STEP** as you **ascend** the scale, but while **descending** the scale return to the **Natural Minor Scale**.

C♭ MAJOR SCALE = 7 FLATS = B♭, E♭, A♭, D♭, G♭, C♭, F♭

(The C♭ Major Scale uses the same notes as the B Major Scale – "Enharmonic")

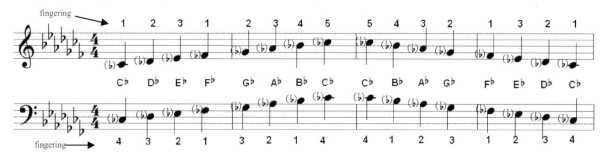

NOTES OF THE SCALE:	C♭	D♭	E♭	F♭	G♭	A♭	B♭	C♭
DEGREES OF THE SCALE:	1	2	3	4	5	6	7	8
TECHNICAL NAMES:	Tonic	Super-tonic	Mediant	Sub-dominant	Dominant	Sub-mediant	Leading Tone	Tonic
FAMILY CHORDS:	C♭	D♭m	E♭m	F♭	G♭ or G♭7	A♭m	B♭dim	
(Most Important HIGHLIGHTED):	(I)	(ii)	(iii)	(IV)	(V or V7)	(vi)	(vii°)	

A♭ NATURAL MINOR SCALE (Relative of C♭ Major) = 7 FLATS = B♭, E♭, A♭, D♭, G♭, C♭, F♭ (The A♭ Natural Scale uses the same notes as the G# Minor Scale – "Enharmonic")

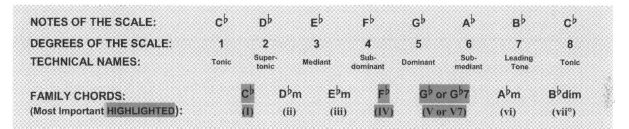

NOTES OF THE SCALE:	A♭	B♭	C♭	D♭	E♭	F♭	G♭	A♭
DEGREES OF THE SCALE:	1	2	3	4	5	6	7	8
TECHNICAL NAMES:	Tonic	Super-tonic	Mediant	Sub-dominant	Dominant	Sub-mediant	Leading Tone	Tonic
FAMILY CHORDS:	A♭m	B♭dim	C♭	D♭m	E♭m, E♭, or E♭7	F♭	G♭	
(Most Important HIGHLIGHTED):	(i)	(ii°)	(III)	(iv)	(v, V, or V7)	(VI)	(VII)	

A♭ HARMONIC MINOR SCALE:

RAISE the 7th note of the scale ½ STEP both **ascending** and **descending** the scale.

A♭ MELODIC MINOR SCALE:

RAISE both the **6th** and **7th** notes of the scale ½ STEP as you **ascend** the scale, but while **descending** the scale return to the **Natural Minor Scale**.

ADDENDUM 1
MAJOR AND MINOR SCALES

NOTES

ADDENDUM 2

MOST IMPORTANT CHORDS REFERENCE SHEETS

NOTES

Chord Piano Is Fun!

ADDENDUM 2
MOST IMPORTANT CHORDS REFERENCE SHEETS
Refer to *Lessons 7, 8 and 12*

Practice the following pages in two different ways:

1. As Root Chords **(Root Cadence Form)**

2. As Inversions **(Inversion Cadence Form)**

Use the following pattern:

I Chord
then
IV Chord
then
I Chord
then
V Chord
then
I Chord
then
V^7 Chord
then
I Chord

Simplified:

I
IV
I
V
I
V^7
I

You will notice that all sets of chords played like this "feel" the same – have basically the same "form" that you feel with your fingers.

As you practice like this you will become more and more proficient at all of your chords!

MOST IMPORTANT CHORDS REFERENCE SHEETS
ALL MAJOR KEYS – ROOT POSITION

I	IV	V	V^7	
(1)	(4)	(5)	(5^7)	
Key of C:	**C** (C E G)	**F** (F A C)	**G** (G B D)	**G**^{7} (G B D F)

SHARP KEYS

	I	IV	V	V^7
	(1)	(4)	(5)	(5^7)
Key of G:	**G** (G B D)	**C** (C E G)	**D** (D F# A)	**D**^{7} (D F# A C)
Key of D:	**D** (D F# A)	**G** (G B D)	**A** (A C# E)	**A**^{7} (A C# E G)
Key of A:	**A** (A C# E)	**D** (D F# A)	**E** (E G# B)	**E**^{7} (E G# B D)
Key of E:	**E** (E G# B)	**A** (A C# E)	**B** (B D# F#)	**B**^{7} (B D# F# A)
Key of B:	**B** (B D# F#)	**E** (E G# B)	**F#** (F# A# C#)	**F#**^{7} (F# A# C# E)
Key of F#:	**F#** (F# A# C#)	**B** (B D# F#)	**C#** (C# E# G#)	**C#**^{7} (C# E# G# B)
(has the same notes as G♭ Chord)				
Key of C#:	**C#** (C# E# G)	**F#** (F# A# C#)	**G#** (G# B# D#)	**G#**^{7} (G# B# D# F#)
(has the same notes as D♭ Chord)				

FLAT KEYS

	I	IV	V	V^7
	(1)	(4)	(5)	(5^7)
Key of F:	**F** (F A C)	**B♭** (B♭ D F)	**C** (C E G)	**C**^{7} (C E G B♭)
Key of B♭:	**B♭** (B♭ D F)	**E♭** (E♭ G B♭)	**F** (F A C)	**F**^{7} (F A C E♭)
Key of E♭:	**E♭** (E♭ G B♭)	**A♭** (A♭ C E♭)	**B♭** (B♭ D F)	**B♭**^{7} (B♭ D F A♭)
Key of A♭:	**A♭** (A♭ C E♭)	**D♭** (D♭ F A♭)	**E♭** (E♭ G B♭)	**E♭**^{7} (E♭ G B♭ D♭)
Key of D♭:	**D♭** (D♭ F A♭)	**G♭** (G♭ B♭ D♭)	**A♭** (A♭ C E♭)	**A♭**^{7} (A♭ C E♭ G♭)
(has the same notes as C# Chord)				
Key of G♭:	**G♭** (G♭ B♭ D♭)	**C♭** (C♭ E♭ G♭)	**D♭** (D♭ F A♭)	**D♭**^{7} (D♭ F A♭ C♭)
(has the same notes as F# Chord)				
Key of C♭:	**C♭** (C♭ E♭ G♭)	**F♭** (F♭ A♭ C♭)	**G♭** (G♭ B♭ D♭)	**G♭**^{7} (G♭ B♭ D♭ F♭)

MOST IMPORTANT CHORDS REFERENCE SHEETS
ALL MAJOR KEYS – INVERSIONS

	I (1)	IV (4)	V (5)	V^7 (dropped 5th) (5^7)
Key of C:	**C** (C E G)	**F** (C F A)	**G** (B D G)	**G**^{7} (B F G)

SHARP KEYS

	I (1)	IV (4)	V (5)	V^7 (dropped 5th) (5^7)
Key of G:	**G** (G B D)	**C** (G C E)	**D** (F# A D)	**D**^{7} (F# C D)
Key of D:	**D** (D F# A)	**G** (D G B)	**A** (C# E A)	**A**^{7} (C# G A)
Key of A:	**A** (A C# E)	**D** (A D F#)	**E** (G# B E)	**E**^{7} (G# D E)
Key of E:	**E** (E G# B)	**A** (E A C#)	**B** (D# F# B)	**B**^{7} (D# A B)
Key of B:	**B** (B D# F#)	**E** (B E G#)	**F#** (A# C# F#)	**F#**^{7} (A# E F#)
Key of F#: (has the same notes as G♭ Chord)	**F#** (F# A# C#)	**B** (F# B D#)	**C#** (E# G# C#)	**C#**^{7} (E# B C#)
Key of C#: (has the same notes as D♭ Chord)	**C#** (C# E# G)	**F#** (C# F# A#)	**G#** (B# D# G#)	**G#**^{7} (B# F# G#)

FLAT KEYS

	I (1)	IV (4)	V (5)	V^7 (dropped 5th) (5^7)
Key of F:	**F** (F A C)	**B♭** (F B♭ D)	**C** (E G C)	**C**^{7} (E B♭ C)
Key of B♭:	**B♭** (B♭ D F)	**E♭** (B♭ E♭ G)	**F** (A C F)	**F**^{7} (A E♭ F)
Key of E♭:	**E♭** (E♭ G B♭)	**A♭** (E♭ A♭ C)	**B♭** (D F B♭)	**B♭**^{7} (D A♭ B♭)
Key of A♭:	**A♭** (A♭ C E♭)	**D♭** (A♭ D♭ F)	**E♭** (G B♭ E♭)	**E♭**^{7} (G D♭ E♭)
Key of D♭: (has the same notes as C# Chord)	**D♭** (D♭ F A♭)	**G♭** (D♭ G♭ B♭)	**A♭** (C E♭ A♭)	**A♭**^{7} (C G♭ A♭)
Key of G♭: (has the same notes as F# Chord)	**G♭** (G♭ B♭ D♭)	**C♭** (G♭ C♭ E♭)	**D♭** (F A♭ D♭)	**D♭**^{7} (F C♭ D♭)
Key of C♭:	**C♭** (C♭ E♭ G♭)	**F♭** (C♭ F♭ A♭)	**G♭** (B♭ D♭ G♭)	**G♭**^{7} (B♭ F♭ G♭)

QUICK REFERENCE SHEET
MOST IMPORTANT CHORDS ALL MAJOR KEYS

	I (1)	IV (4)	V (5)	V^7 (5^7)
KEY:				
C:	C	F	G	G^7

SHARP KEYS:

	I (1)	IV (4)	V (5)	V^7 (5^7)
KEY:				
G:	G	C	D	D^7
D:	D	G	A	A^7
A:	A	D	E	E^7
E:	E	A	B	B^7
B:	B	E	F#	$F\#^7$
F#:	F#	B	C#	$C\#^7$
C#:	C#	F#	G#	$G\#^7$

FLAT KEYS:

	I (1)	IV (4)	V (5)	V^7 (5^7)
KEY:				
F:	F	B♭	C	C^7
B♭:	B♭	E♭	F	F^7
E♭:	E♭	A♭	B♭	$B♭^7$
D♭:	D♭	G♭	A♭	$A♭^7$
A♭:	A♭	D♭	E♭	$E♭^7$
G♭:	G♭	C♭	D♭	$D♭^7$
C♭:	C♭	F♭	G♭	$G♭^7$

MOST IMPORTANT CHORDS REFERENCE SHEETS
ALL MINOR KEYS – ROOT CHORDS

	i (1)	iv (4)	V (5)	V^7 (5^7)
A Minor:	**Am** (A C E)	**Dm** (D F A)	**E** (E G# B)	E^7 (E G# B D)

SHARP KEYS

	i (1)	iv (4)	V (5)	V^7 (5^7)
E Minor:	**Em** (E G B)	**Am** (A C E)	**B** (B D# F#)	B^7 (B D# F# A)
B Minor:	**Bm** (B D F#)	**Em** (E G B)	**F#** (F# A# C#)	$F\#^7$ (F# A# C# E)
F# Minor: (uses the same chords as Gb Minor)	**F#m** (F# A C#)	**Bm** (B D F#)	**C#** (C# E# G#)	$C\#^7$ (C# E# G# B)
C# Minor:	**C#m** (C#, E, G#)	**F#m** (F# A C#)	**G#** (G# B# D#)	$G\#^7$ (G# B D# F)
G# Minor: (uses the same chords as A♭ Minor)	**G#m** (G# B D#)	**C#m** (C#, E, G#)	**D#** (D# F## A#) (G)	$D\#^7$ (D# F## A# C) (G)
D# Minor: (uses the same chords as E♭ Minor)	**D#m** (D# F# A#)	**G#m** (G#, B, D#)	**A#** (A# C## E#) (D) (F)	$A\#^7$ (A# C## E# G#) (D) (F)
A# Minor: (uses the same chords as Bb Minor)	**A#m** (A# C# E#)	**D#m** (D#, F#, A#)	**E#** (E# G## B#) (F) (A) (C)	$E\#^7$ (E# G## B# D#) (F) (A) (C)

FLAT KEYS

	i (1)	iv (4)	V (5)	V^7 (5^7)
D Minor:	**Dm** (D F A)	**Gm** (G B♭ D)	**A** (A C# E)	A^7 (A C# E G)
G Minor:	**Gm** (G B♭ D)	**Cm** (C E♭ G)	**D** (D F# A)	D^7 (D F# A C)
C Minor:	**Cm** (C E♭ G)	**Fm** (F A♭ C)	**G** (G B D)	G^7 (G B D F)
F Minor:	**Fm** (F A♭ C)	**B♭m** (B♭ D♭ F)	**C** (C E G)	C^7 (C E G B♭)
B♭ Minor: (uses the same chords as A# Minor)	**B♭m** (B♭ D♭ F)	**E♭m** (E♭ G♭ B♭)	**F** (F A C)	F^7 (F A C E♭)
E♭ Minor: (uses the same chords as D# Minor)	**E♭m** (E♭ G♭ B♭)	**A♭m** (A♭ C♭ E♭)	**B♭** (B♭ D F)	$B♭^7$ (B♭ D F A♭)
A♭ Minor: (uses the same chords G# Minor)	**A♭m** (A♭ C♭ E♭) (B)	**D♭m** (D♭ F♭ A♭) (E)	**E♭** (E♭ G B♭)	$E♭^7$ (E♭ G B♭ D♭)

MOST IMPORTANT CHORDS REFERENCE SHEETS
ALL MINOR KEYS – INVERSIONS

	i (1)	**iv** (4)	**V** (5)	**V**^{7} (dropped 5th) (5^7)
A Minor:	**Am** (A C E)	**Dm** (A D F)	**E** (G# B E)	**E**^{7} (G# D E)

SHARP KEYS

	i (1)	**iv** (4)	**V** (5)	**V**^{7} (dropped 5th) (5^7)
E Minor:	**Em** (E G B)	**Am** (E A C)	**B** (D# F# B)	**B**^{7} (D# A B)
B Minor:	**Bm** (B D F#)	**Em** (B E G)	**F#** (A# C# F#)	**F#**^{7} (A# E F#)
F# Minor:	**F#m** (F# A C#)	**Bm** (F# B D)	**C#** (E# G# C#) (F)	**C#**^{7} (E# B C#) (F)

(uses the same chords as Gb Minor)

	i	**iv**	**V**	**V**^{7}
C# Minor:	**C#m** (C#, E, G#)	**F#m** (C# F# A)	**G#** (B# D# G#)	**G#**^{7} (B F G#)
G# Minor:	**G#m** (G# B D#)	**C#m** (G# C# E)	**D#** (F## A# D#) (G)	**D#**^{7} (F## C# D#) (G)

(uses the same chords as A♭ Minor)

	i	**iv**	**V**	**V**^{7}
D# Minor:	**D#m** (D# F# A#)	**G#m** (D# G# B)	**A#** (C## E# A#) (D) (F)	**A#**^{7} (C## G# A#) (D)

(uses the same chords as E♭ Minor)

	i	**iv**	**V**	**V**^{7}
A# Minor:	**A#m** (A# C# E#)	**D#m** (A# D# F#)	**E#** (G## B# E#) (A) (C) (F)	**E#**^{7} (G## D# E#) (A) (F)

(uses the same chords as Bb Minor)

FLAT KEYS

	i (1)	**iv** (4)	**V** (5)	**V**^{7} (dropped 5th) (5^7)
D Minor:	**Dm** (D F A)	**Gm** (D G B♭)	**A** (C# E A)	**A**^{7} (C# G A)
G Minor:	**Gm** (G B♭ D)	**Cm** (G C E♭)	**D** (F# A D)	**D**^{7} (F# C D)
C Minor:	**Cm** (C E♭ G)	**Fm** (C F A♭)	**G** (B D G)	**G**^{7} (B F G)
F Minor:	**Fm** (F A♭ C)	**B♭m** (F B♭ D♭)	**C** (E G C)	**C**^{7} (E B♭ C)
B♭ Minor:	**B♭m** (B♭ D♭ F)	**E♭m** (B♭ E♭ G♭)	**F** (A C F)	**F**^{7} (A E♭ F)

(uses the same chords as A# Minor)

	i	**iv**	**V**	**V**^{7}
E♭ Minor	**E♭m** (E♭ G♭ B♭)	**A♭m** (E♭ A♭ C♭) (B)	**B♭** (D F B♭)	**B♭**^{7} (D A♭ B♭)

(uses the same chords as D# Minor)

	i	**iv**	**V**	**V**^{7}
A♭ Minor:	**A♭m** (A♭ C♭ E♭) (B)	**D♭m** (A♭ D♭ F♭) (E)	**E♭** (G B♭ E♭)	**E♭**^{7} (G D♭ E♭)

(uses the same chords G# Minor)

QUICK REFERENCE SHEET
MOST IMPORTANT CHORDS ALL MINOR KEYS

	i	iv	V	V^7
	(1)	(4)	(5)	(5^7)
KEY:				
A Minor:	Am	Dm	E	E^7

SHARP KEYS:

	i	iv	V	V^7
	(1)	(4)	(5)	(5^7)
KEY:				
E Minor:	Em	Am	B	B^7
B Minor:	Bm	Em	F#	$F\#^7$
F# Minor: (uses the same chords as G♭ Minor)	F#m	Bm	C#	$C\#^7$
C# Minor: (uses the same chords as D♭ Minor)	C#m	F#m	G#	$G\#^7$
G# Minor: (uses the same chords as A♭ Minor)	G#m	C#m	D#	$D\#^7$
D# Minor:	D#m	G#m	D#	$A\#^7$
A# Minor:	A#m	D#m	E#	$E\#^7$

FLAT KEYS:

	i	iv	V	V^7
	(1)	(4)	(5)	(5^7)
KEY:				
D Minor:	Dm	Gm	A	A^7
G Minor:	Gm	Cm	D	D^7
C Minor:	Cm	Fm	G	G^7
F Minor:	Fm	B♭m	C	C^7
B♭ Minor:	B♭m	E♭m	F	F7
E♭ Minor	E♭m	A♭m	B♭	$B♭^7$
A♭ Minor:	A♭m	D♭m	E♭	$E♭^7$

NOTES

ADDENDUM 3

BUILDING ALL CHORDS
REFERENCE SHEETS

NOTES

BUILDING ALL CHORDS

Refer to *Lesson 24* – *Building Other Types of Chords*

Chord Type	Abbreviation	Examples	Spelling of Chord	Sample (in Key of C)
Major	* none M Maj △	C CM Cmaj C △	1+3+5	C-E-G
Minor	m, –, min	Cm C— C min	1+$^\flat$3+5	C-E$^\flat$-G
Diminished	dim °	Cdim C°	1+$^\flat$3+$^\flat$5	C-E$^\flat$-G$^\flat$
Augmented	aug,+	Caug C+	1+3+#5	C-E-G#
Suspended 4th	4 sus sus4	C4 Csus Csus4	1+4+5	C-F-G
Suspended 2nd	sus2	Csus2	1+2+5	C-D-G

7th Chords				
Chord Type	Abbreviation	Examples	Spelling of Chord	Sample (in Key of C)
7th (Dominant 7th)	7	C7	1+3+5+$^\flat$7	C-E-G-B$^\flat$
Minor 7th	m7 –7 min7	Cm7 C—7 Cmin7	1+$^\flat$3+5+$^\flat$7	C-E$^\flat$-G-B$^\flat$

Chord Type	Abbreviation	Examples	Spelling of Chord	Sample (in Key of C)
Major 7th	M7 Maj7 △7	CM7 CMaj7 C△7	1+3+5	C-E-G
Diminished 7th	dim7 °7	Cdim7 C°7	1+$\flat$3+ $\flat$5+$\flat\flat$7	C-E$\flat$-G$\flat$-B$\flat\flat$ (A)
Augmented 7th	aug7 +7	Caug7 C+7	1+3+#5+$\flat$7	C-E-G#-B$\flat$
Augmented Major 7th	aug7+ maj7+ M7#5 M7+	Caug7+ Cmaj7+ CM7#5 CM7+	1+3+#5+7	C-E-G#-B
Suspended 7th	sus7	sus7	1+4+5+$\flat$7	C-F-G-B$\flat$
Major7th, Flat 5th	maj7$\flat$5 M 7$\flat$5	Cmaj7$\flat$5 CM 7$\flat$5	1+3+$\flat$5+7	C-E-G$\flat$-B
Major7th, Flat 9th	maj7$\flat$9 M 7$\flat$9	Cmaj7$\flat$9 CM 7$\flat$9	1+3+$\flat$5+7+$\flat$9	C-E-G$\flat$-B-D$\flat$
7th, flat 9th	7$\flat$9	C7$\flat$9	1+3+5+$\flat$7+$\flat$9	C-E-G-B$\flat$-D$\flat$
7th, sharp 9th	7#9	C7#9	1+3+5+$\flat$7+#9	C-E-G-B$\flat$-D#
7th, Flat 5th	7$\flat$9	C7$\flat$5	1+3 $\flat$5+$\flat$7	C-E-G$\flat$-B$\flat$
7th, flat 5th, sharp 9th	7$\flat$5#9	C7$\flat$5#9	1+3+$\flat$5+$\flat$7+#9	C-E-G$\flat$-B$\flat$-D#
Minor, Major 7th	min/Maj7 min(M7) — (maj7)	Cmin/Maj7 Cmin(M7) C— (maj7)	1+$\flat$3+5+7	C-E$\flat$-G-B
Minor 7th, Flat 5th (**Half-diminished 7th**)	min7$\flat$5	Cmin7$\flat$5	1+ $\flat$3+$\flat$5+$\flat$7	C-E$\flat$-G$\flat$-B$\flat$

6th Chords

Chord Type	Abbreviation	Examples	Spelling of Chord	Sample (in Key of C)
6th	6	C6	1+3+5+6	C-E-G-A
Minor 6th	min6	Cmin6	1+$\flat$3+ 5+6	C-E$\flat$-G-A
6, 9	6/9	C6/9	1+3+5+6+9	C-E-G-A-D
Minor 6th, 9	m6/9 −6/9	Cm6/9 C−6/9	1+$\flat$3+5+6+9	C-E$\flat$-G-A-D

9th Chords

Chord Type	Abbreviation	Examples	Spelling of Chord	Sample (in Key of C)
9th	9	C9	1+3+5+$\flat$7+9	C-E-G-B$\flat$-D
Major 9th	maj9 △9	Cmaj9 C△9	1+3+5+7+9	C-E-G-B-D
Minor 9th	M9 −9	CM9 C−9	1+$\flat$3+5+$\flat$7+9	C-E$\flat$-G-B$\flat$-D
Suspended 9th	sus9	sus9	1+4+5+$\flat$7+9	C-F-G-B$\flat$-D
Augmented 9th	aug 9 +9	Caug 9 C+9	1+3+#5+$\flat$7+9	C-E-G#-B$\flat$-D
Augmented major 9th	maj9+	Cmaj9+	1+3+#5+7+9	C-E-G#-B-D

Chord Type	Abbreviation	Examples	Spelling of Chord	Sample (in Key of C)
minor, Major 9th	min/Maj9 –(maj9) mM9	Cmin/Maj9 C–(maj9), CmM9	1+♭3+5+7+9	C-E♭-G-B-D
9th, Flat 5th	9♭5	C9♭5	1+3+♭5+♭7+9	C-E-G♭-B♭-D
Major 9th, sharp 11th	maj9#11	Cmaj9#11	1+3+5+7+9+#11	C-E-G-B-D-F#
9th, #11th	9#11	C9#11	1+3+5+♭7+9+#11	C-E-G-B♭-D-F#

11th Chords

Chord Type	Abbreviation	Examples	Spelling of Chord	Sample (in Key of C)
11th	11	C11	1+5+♭7+9+11	C-G-B♭-D-F
Major 11th	maj11 △11	Cmaj11 C△11	1+3+5+7+9+11	C-E-G-B-D-F
Minor 11th	m11 min 11	Cm11 min 11	1+♭3+5+♭7+9+11	C-E♭-G-B♭-D-F
Suspended 11th	sus11	sus11	1+4+5+♭7+9+11	C-F-G-B♭-D+F
Augmented 11th	aug 11 +11	Caug 11 C+11	1+3+#5+♭7+9+11	C-E-G#-B♭-D-F
Augmented major 11th	maj11+	Cmaj11+	1+3+#5+7+9+11	C-E-G#-B-D-F
minor, Major 11th	min/Maj11 –(maj11) mM11	Cmin/Maj11 C–(maj11), CmM11	1+♭3+5+7+9+11	C-E♭-G-B-D-F
11th, Flat 5th	11♭5	C11♭5	1+3+♭5+♭7+9+11	C-E-G♭-B♭-D-F

13th Chords

Chord Type	Abbreviation	Examples	Spelling of Chord	Sample (in Key of C)
13th	13	C13	1+5+♭7+9+11+13	C-G-B♭-D-F-A
Major 13th	maj13 △13	Cmaj13 c△13	1+3+5+7+9+11+13	C-E-G-B-D-F-A
Minor 13th	m13 min 13	Cm13 min 13	1+♭3+5+♭7+9+11+13	C-E♭-G-B♭-D-F-A
Suspended 13th	sus13	sus13	1+4+5+♭7+9+11+13	C-F-G-B♭-D-F-A
Augmented 13th	aug 13 +13	Caug 13 C+13	1+3+#5+♭7+9+11+13	C-E-G#-B♭-D-F-A
Augmented major 13th	maj13+	Cmaj13+	1+3+#5+7+9+11+13	C-E-G#-B-D-F-A
minor, Major 13th	min/Maj13 –(maj13) mM13	Cmin/Maj13 C–(maj13), CmM13	1+♭3+5+7+9+11+13	C-E♭-G-B-D-F-A
13th, Flat 5th	13♭5	C13♭5	1+3+♭5+♭7+9+11+13	C-E-G♭-B♭-D-F-A

*   Any chord without any type of notation after it is a "Major Chord" (as in "C").

NOTES

ADDENDUM 4

MAJOR CIRCLE OF 5THS, 4THS

NOTES

THE MAJOR CIRCLE OF 5THS/4THS
USE TO LOCATE AND PRACTICE THE "MOST IMPORTANT CHORDS"

The following is the **Circle of 5ths/Circle of 4ths**. This is a great tool to use to practice your chords. The **Circle of 5ths/4ths** is used in music to show **relationship** between the **KEYS** and also between the **CHORDS**.

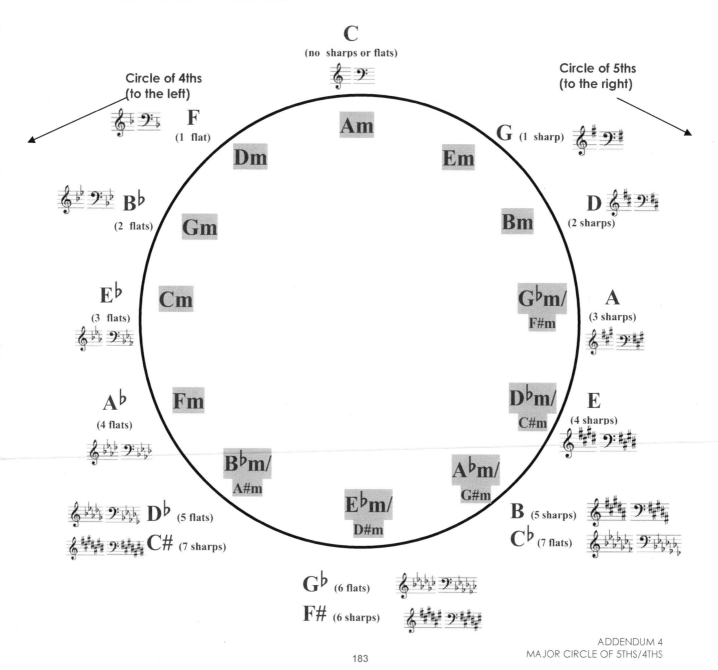

WHAT IS THE CIRCLE OF 5THS/CIRCLE OF 4THS?

The **Circle of 5ths/4ths** is used in music to show **relationship** between the **KEYS** and also between the **CHORDS**.

If you notice, if you start at the top from "C" and go around to the **RIGHT** of the circle, the "G" is **5 notes** from "C", the "D" is 5 notes from "G", etc. This continues all the way around the **RIGHT** of the circle. Thus the name **"Circle of 5ths"**.

If you start from C and go to the **LEFT**, you will find that each of these notes is **4 notes** from the previous note. Thus the name **"Circle of 4ths"**.

The **note** on the **outside** of the circle is the **Key**, and also the name of the **Root Chord** for that key.

The **note** on the **inside** of the circle is the **Relative Minor Key**, which has the same key signature as the MAJOR Key on the outside of the circle. This is also the name of the Root Major Chord for that Key. For example, the Relative Minor Key to the Key of C is "**Am**" (see inside of the circle beneath it), and the Relative Minor Key to the Key of A♭ is **Fm** (see inside of circle to the right of it).   (See **Addendum 5 – Minor Circle of 5ᵗʰ/4ths** for more explanation.)

HOW DO I USE THE CIRCLE OF 5THS/4THS?

You can use this circle to find your chords. To find the **"MOST IMPORTANT CHORDS"** for each key, locate the key in which the song is written (for example, the **Key of C**). One notch to the **LEFT** of this key/chord (moving in the direction of "Circle of 4ᵗʰˢ") is "F" which is the **4 (IV) chord** of the key of C. Moving one notch to the **RIGHT** of this key/chord, (moving in the direction of "**Circle of 5ᵗʰˢ**") is "**G**", which is the **5 (V) chord** of the Key of C. This is how you find the **Most Important Chords** by the Circle of 5ths/4ths.

You can also use this circle to practice your scales. Just start at "**C**" and practice the "**C Scale**" then move to the right or to the left and practice each scale around the circle. (Refer to **Addendum 1 – Major and Minor Scales** for notes in the scales and fingering.)

This is a great tool to use, and one to be familiar with and get to know!

ADDENDUM 5

MINOR CIRCLE
OF 5THS, 4THS

NOTES

THE MINOR CIRCLE OF 5THS/4THS

The following is the **Minor Circle of 5ths/4ths**. Just like the **Circle of 5ths/4ths**, it shows the **relationship** between both the Key and Chord of each Minor Scale/Key. (**See Addendum 4 – Circle of 5ths/4ths.**)

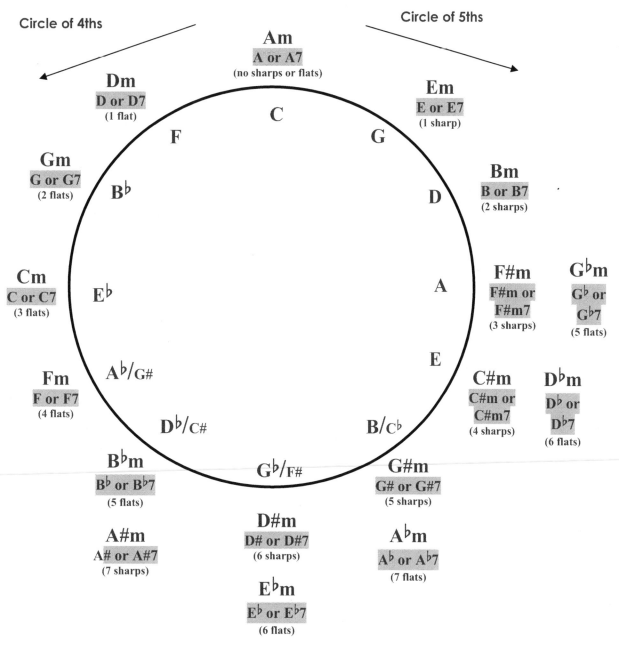

Circle of 4ths

Circle of 5ths

Am
A or A7
(no sharps or flats)

Dm
D or D7
(1 flat)

Em
E or E7
(1 sharp)

Gm
G or G7
(2 flats)

Bm
B or B7
(2 sharps)

Cm
C or C7
(3 flats)

F#m
F#m or F#m7
(3 sharps)

G♭m
G♭ or G♭7
(5 flats)

Fm
F or F7
(4 flats)

C#m
C#m or C#m7
(4 sharps)

D♭m
D♭ or D♭7
(6 flats)

B♭m
B♭ or B♭7
(5 flats)

G#m
G# or G#7
(5 sharps)

A#m
A# or A#7
(7 sharps)

D#m
D# or D#7
(6 sharps)

A♭m
A♭ or A♭7
(7 flats)

E♭m
E♭ or E♭7
(6 flats)

Circle interior labels: C, F, G, B♭, D, E♭, A, A♭/G#, E, D♭/C#, B/C♭, G♭/F#

Chord Piano Is Fun!

HOW DO I USE THE MINOR CIRCLE OF 5THS/4THS?

The note on the **outside** of the circle, is the **Minor Key** and the **Root Chord** for that Key. The highlighted chords are the chords that you would use if you were using the **5 (V) chord** or **5^7** (**V^7**) in that Minor Key (**see *Lesson 19 – Minor Key Family Chords***).

For example, if you want to find the **chord family** for the **Key of A Minor**, find **Am**, which is the **1 (I)** Chord for this Key, then go to the **left** one notch (in the direction of the "Circle of 4ths") for the **4 (iv)** chord (**Dm**), and go to the **right** one notch (in the direction of the "Circle of 5ths") for the **5 (V)** chord (**Em**), **but use the highlighted chord (E or E7).** (*This note should be a **MAJOR** chord, so adjust the minor chord to be either the major chord or the 7th chord.*)

The notes on the **inside** of the circle, are the **RELATIVE MAJOR SCALES/KEYS** (refer to ***Lesson 18 – Minor Scales***), that have the same key signatures as the Minor Keys above it.

You can also use this circle to practice your Minor Scales. Just start at "**Am**" and practice the "**A Minor Scale**" then move to the right or to the left and practice each scale around the circle. (Refer to ***Addendum 1 – Major and Minor Scales*** for notes in the scales and fingering.)

This is a great tool to use, and one to be familiar with and get to know!

ADDENDUM 6

THE BLUES

BLUES FORM, SCALES AND CHORDS

NOTES

Remember the **Blues Form** (From Lesson 26):

Number of bars	Chord
4	I^7
2	IV^7
2	I^7
1	V^7
1	IV^7
2	I^7

THE BLUES
Refer to *Lesson 26*

Here are the Blues Scales with their suggested fingerings for each key:

KEY OF C

Chords to Use: C^7, F^7, AND G^7

SHARP KEYS

KEY OF G

Chords to Use: G^7, C^7, AND D^7

KEY OF D

Chords to Use: D^7, G^7, AND A^7

Chord Piano Is Fun!

KEY OF A

A C D E♭ E G A G E E♭ D C A

Chords to Use: A⁷, D⁷, AND E⁷

KEY OF E

E G A B♭ B D E D B B♭ A G E

Chords to Use: E⁷, A⁷, AND B⁷

KEY OF B

B D E F F# A B A F# F E D B

Chords to Use: B⁷, E⁷, AND F#⁷

FLAT KEYS

KEY OF F

Chords to Use: F⁷ , B♭⁷, AND C⁷

KEY OF B♭

Chords to Use: B♭⁷ , E♭⁷, AND F⁷

KEY OF E♭

Chords to Use: E♭⁷ , A♭⁷, AND B♭⁷

Chord Piano Is Fun!

KEY OF A♭

(Shown with "enharmonics" (for example) "B" instead of "C♭" – this makes it easier to read/play)

A♭ B   D♭ D   E♭ G♭ A♭ G♭   E♭ D   D♭ B   A♭
    (C♭)   (C♭)

Chords to Use: A♭7 , D♭7 , AND E♭7

KEY OF D♭

(Shown with "enharmonics" (for example) "E" instead of "F♭" – this makes it easier to read/play)

D♭ E   G♭ G   A♭ B   D♭ B   A♭ G   G♭ E   D♭
    (F♭)   (F♭)

Chords to Use: D♭7 , G♭7 , AND A♭7

KEY OF G♭

(Shown with "enharmonics" (for example) "A" instead of "B♭♭" – this makes it easier to read/play)

G♭   A   B   C   D♭ E   G♭ E   D♭ C   B   A   G♭
    (B♭♭) (C♭) (D♭♭)   (F♭)   (F♭)   (D♭♭) (C♭) (B♭♭)

Chords to Use: G♭7 , C♭7 , AND D♭7

Chord Piano Is Fun!

Made in the USA
Columbia, SC
13 July 2018